T0072456

Cambridge Elements ≡

Elements in Publishing and Book Culture
edited by
Samantha Rayner
University College London
Leah Tether
University of Bristol

WOMEN AND LETTERPRESS PRINTING 1920–2020

Gendered Impressions

Claire Battershill
University of Toronto

CAMBRIDGE
UNIVERSITY PRESS

CAMBRIDGE
UNIVERSITY PRESS

University Printing House, Cambridge CB2 8BS, United Kingdom

One Liberty Plaza, 20th Floor, New York, NY 10006, USA

477 Williamstown Road, Port Melbourne, VIC 3207, Australia

314–321, 3rd Floor, Plot 3, Splendor Forum, Jasola District Centre,
New Delhi – 110025, India

103 Penang Road, #05–06/07, Visioncrest Commercial, Singapore 238467

Cambridge University Press is part of the University of Cambridge.

It furthers the University's mission by disseminating knowledge in the pursuit of
education, learning, and research at the highest international levels of excellence.

www.cambridge.org
Information on this title: www.cambridge.org/9781009219327
DOI: 10.1017/9781009219365

First published 2022

A catalogue record for this publication is available from the British Library.

ISBN 978-1-009-21932-7 Paperback
ISSN 2514-8524 (online)
ISSN 2514-8516 (print)

Women and Letterpress Printing 1920–2020

Gendered Impressions

Elements in Publishing and Book Culture

DOI: 10.1017/9781009219365
First published online: May 2022

Claire Battershill
University of Toronto

Author for correspondence: Claire Battershill, claire.battershill@utoronto.ca

ABSTRACT: This Element analyzes the relationship between gender and literary letterpress printing from the early twentieth century to the beginning of the twenty-first. Drawing on examples from modernist writer/printers of the 1920s to literary book artists of the early twenty-first century, it offers a way of thinking about the feminist historiography of printing as we confront the presence and particular character of letterpress in a digital age.

This Element is divided into four sections: the first, 'Historicizing', traces the critical histories of women and print through to the twentieth and twenty-first centuries. The second section, 'Learning', offers an analysis of some of the modes of discourse and training through which women and gender minorities have learned the craft of printing. The third section, 'Individualizing', offers brief biographical vignettes. The fourth section, 'Writing', focusses on printers' own written reflections about letterpress. This title is also available as Open Access on Cambridge Core.

KEYWORDS: book history, letterpress, feminism, women's history, literary printing

ISBNs: 9781009219327 (PB), 9781009219365 (OC)
ISSNs: 2514-8524 (online), 2514-8516 (print)

Contents

Preface

This story begins in a rather unexpected place, with an unlikely figure for a study of women and the art of letterpress printing. Robertson Davies was a Canadian novelist and the first Master of Massey College in Toronto, Canada. A gruff old fellow with a formidable beard, he was a celebrated writer and by all accounts a hilarious storyteller – but he was no feminist. For the first nine years of his time as the Master of Massey College (1963–81), in fact, the institution only admitted men.[1] He acquired printing presses for the college, with the intention that the students might use them to print their own writings, and so were born the 'Quadrats'[2] – a group of professional typographers, printers, and bibliophiles who built a small society and an impressive collection of printing materials, ephemera, and antique equipment.[3] It was in this space, called The Bibliography Room, where I first learned how to print, in 2008, alongside other novice printers – mostly women.[4] I spent nearly every Thursday afternoon during the five years of my PhD programme in an informal apprenticeship[5] learning how to set **metal**

---

[1] The first female fellows were admitted to the college in 1974. For a detailed history of Massey College, see Skelton, *A Meeting of Minds*.

[2] For a history of the Quadrats and a list of members, see Skelton, *A Meeting of Minds*, pp. 126–8.

[3] For all instances of specialist printing terminology, I either define these in plain language within the text or indicate these in bold and include them in the Glossary at the end of the Element for reference. 'Quadrat' in this context is a printing play on words, referring triply to a small unit of spacing used to make up a line of type, to a square used in ecology to define the boundaries of a specific area of study, and to the architectural space of the college 'quadrangle' that forms an enclosed spatial centre associated with academic life.

[4] My contemporaries 2008–12 were Lindsey Eckert and Heather Jessup. I was taught by the college librarian, Marie Korey, and the college printers, first Brian Maloney and then Nelson Adams.

[5] During my time at Massey, the apprenticeship programme was formalized and it continues now with new 'printing fellows' joining each year. Please see 'Printing Fellowship Program' for full curricular details and names of apprentices. For a student's account of the experience of learning in The Bibliography Room and further details of the printing equipment and its provenance, see King, 'Grab an

type, how to clean and preserve **wood** type, how to sort **spacing** by size, how to produce prints on a variety of different nineteenth-century cast-iron **hand presses**, and how to tell the stories of those presses for interested passers-by. Mostly, I made ephemeral prints such as bookmarks and event keepsakes and quartos for use in book history graduate seminars.

While I was never a part of the inner circle of 'Quadrats' at Massey, I accessed that space as a female student working on Virginia Woolf's Hogarth Press, open to learning and unaware at the time of the long history and bounded nature of print shops as gendered enclosures. My own interest in Hogarth Press stemmed initially from the hypothesis, also advanced by Hermione Lee, Alice Staveley, and others, that the rhythms and processes of letterpress printing were connected, for Woolf, to her writing.[6] Following Woolf in the 1920s and 1930s, other modernist women writers also took up letterpress printing, notably Nancy Cunard and Laura Riding,[7] and in this Element I aim to enrich some of the context around and extend the narrative from Woolf: through the trade structures that excluded women writers to the other modernist women who also printed and then through to the present moment and to the afterlife of the modernist independent press in contemporary letterpress projects by women.

I recognize here that Woolf is a privileged exception in the world of printing, as I am: quite a lot of nineteenth- and early twentieth-century print history is predicated on the assumption that the writer and the printer would be separate individuals with separate jobs to do. The purpose of trade printing was not the same as acts of printing undertaken by artists or by students. As an apprentice at Massey, however, I had academic, creative, and historical intentions simultaneously. I wanted to learn how to print in part because I thought it might help me think differently about how Woolf wrote but also about how I might write. In learning to set type and to print,

Apron'. For a video tour of The Bibliography Room and an introduction to typesetting, please see Bromberg et al., 'An Introduction to Letterpress Printing'.

[6] My first book, *Modernist Lives*, focusses on a rather different element of the Hogarth Press's operations, its biographical publications.

[7] For more on Riding's print practice, see Kopley, *Virginia Woolf and Poetry* and Börjel, 'The Vampire and the Darling Priest of Modernism'.

I explored the malleable relationship between language, tactility, and time. I therefore, like Johanna Drucker,[8] take as fundamental the idea that letter-press printing is a literary art and an art of textuality. That there is a relationship between the intellectual contents being printed and the act of printing itself, and that this relationship is even more intimate when the writing and the printing are done by the same individual or small collabora-tive group, seems essential in understanding the value of printing as a form of expression undertaken by women writers, activists, and artists in the twen-tieth and twenty-first-centuries. The **lay** of the type case, the sound of the ink on rollers, the sensory and embodied experiences of print, all of these are pleasures and processes that matter to writers who print. The words on the page also matter enough to the writers who produce them that they demand the care, attention, and time required by the slow art of letterpress. Figure 1 is an example of a keepsake produced by Elisa Tersigni, at the time one of the student apprentices in The Bibliography Room, as a commentary on the gendered nature of printing.

In what follows, I will lay out what I see as some of the contours of the rich history of women and letterpress printing in Canada, the United States, and the UK, through the twentieth century and up to 2020. I propose here a number of ways of thinking interdisciplinarily and theoretically about the historiography of women and printing. Throughout, I take an integrative approach, pulling materials from design history, printing history, book history, literary studies, creative writing studies, feminist historiography, and interdisciplinary craft studies.

This Element is organized in four sections. In Section 1, I begin with a methodological reflection on the existing critical discourse on women and printing, an analysis of some of the particular considerations of letterpress's role in a contemporary era, and a reflection on why practitioners might choose this technology now. I continue in Section 2 with an analysis of some of the modes of discourse and training through which women have learned the craft of printing. In this section, I also offer a brief description of the process of letterpress printing itself and its associated terminology, which I read for its gendered linguistic associations. In Section 3, I discuss short vignettes

---

[8] Drucker, 'Letterpress Language'.

Figure 1 'Let Her Press' printed in the Massey College Bibliography
Room by Elisa Tersigni. Photograph by Tim Perry. Reproduced with the
permission of the artist.

focusing on particular examples of women engaged in acts of printing as
representations of gendered labour. Section 4 focusses on printers' own
written reflections about letterpress and particularly about the relationship
that author-printers see between their role as authors and the act of printing.

1 Historicizing

The critical history of women in printing is rich but also rather diffuse. It crosses work in a variety of disciplines: graphic design history, literary studies, book history, labour and political history, and women and gender studies. There are many fascinating individual case studies of societies and collectives, particularly in the period just preceding the one I consider here, such as the Women's Printing Society, the Cuala Press,[9] and the Victoria Press.[10] Often these studies isolate a component of the story: the social structures of trade unions, the mechanics of printing, or a literary analysis of the works on the page. In this Element, I draw from all of these different disciplinary foundations in order to form a method for analysing the ways in which form and craft – as polysemic constructs that cross the boundary between materiality and textuality – can encourage holistic thinking about women and print without oversimplifying a complex and diverse set of individual examples. In this section, I offer an interdisciplinary approach to women and printing that considers the topic from a variety of perspectives.

1.1 Formes and Forms

The focus of this Element is, in one sense, rigorously specific: I write here primarily about letterpress printing and not about other mechanisms by which prints and books can be or have been made in the last 100 years. I do not write here about zines made using photocopiers or **mimeographs**, about mass-produced artefacts, about textual embroidery samplers, or about calligraphy, although all of these are fascinating textual media with growing critical literatures, and many of the questions provoked by letterpress printing might equally apply to bookmaking using other methods.[11] I am interested specifically in understanding what is distinctive about letterpress

---

[9] See Ciara, 'Women of the Cuala Press'.

[10] For an account of women's labour in the seventeenth century, see Coker, 'Gendered Spheres'.

[11] Work on artists' books that use a variety of print technologies is an important source of dialogue for thinking about letterpress. See Drucker's *The Century of Artist's Books* and Weber's *Freedom of the Presses*.

in a time when transferring text in multiple copies onto paper is extremely fast with the use of digital printing and, in some cases, no longer even necessary at all since we frequently now do our reading on screens. To borrow a term more commonly used for newer technologies and in design theory, what are the precise 'affordances' of letterpress for literature during this period of time, and how might those affordances relate to the tangled histories of feminism, aesthetics, and labour in the twentieth and early twenty-first centuries? In order to unpack these various affordances, my specific examples here focus primarily on relatively small operations and the work of a small subgroup of letterpress artists I define, particularly in Section 4, as literary printers.

In her influential book, *Forms* (2015), Caroline Levine begins with a challenge to the critical orthodoxy that a literary critic doing her job ought to 'keep her formalism and her historicism analytically separate'.[12] Instead, Levine posits a framework in which 'forms are at work everywhere'[13] and advocates for a more capacious analysis of social and political structures, literary structures, and material structures all as forms deserving of formalist attention. The idea of form itself has been at the heart of literary critical crises of disciplinary self-representation throughout the period of time I cover in this Element. Formalism's rise in the early twentieth century – via the New Critics such as Eliot and Empson and the Russian Formalists – was initially concerned with the analysis of literary texts on their own terms, stripped of easy explanatory contextual meanings and analysable through close attention to linguistic particulars. Formalism in this sense does not, in most cases, admit the possibility or relevance of material form into the discussion. The 'form' of a poem generally would be more likely to refer to its categorization as sonnet rather than the fact that the **body text** of the edition under consideration is set in 12pt Caslon type. Yet material form and literary form in the cases I discuss in this Element are aligned and allied. Johanna Drucker's study of early twentieth-century experimental typography argues forcefully that 'it is *in* material that the activity of signification is produced',[14] and not only in works that exploit deliberately disruptive

---

[12] Levine, *Forms*, p. 14. [13] Ibid., p. 15. [14] Drucker, *The Visible Word*, p. 4.

or innovative typographical practices. A consideration of all elements of form, literary, linguistic, material, and historical, is merited in a study of textual artefacts and the processes and practices that produced them. The idea of form also finds a material and literal meaning in the printing world in the object of the '**forme**', the ready-to-print object: a metal frame (a **chase**) in which the page layout including type, illustrations, and spacing is locked. A forme is a bounded and constrained space in which almost infinite possibilities have been **locked up** and are ready to print, including all of the various possibilities of literary form. Many letterpress artists, as I will discuss in Section 3, are thinking about both form and forme as they produce their work: they're thinking about language, rhythm, and metaphor just as they are about line length, **justification**, and paper type.

In my frame of reference, letterpress is primarily an artist's, activist's, or writer's medium, as opposed to an instrumental or commercial technology. However, understanding the structural history of labour in printing is crucial to understanding subsequent constructions of gender in twentieth-century print. I therefore address industrial trade history here, particularly in Section 2, in order to demonstrate the forms of exclusionary practices in print shops that inform the work and the experiences of later artists. There is, however, for most of the printers I write about here, significant self-awareness and conscious adoption of this medium for specifically artistic, political, or literary purposes.

1.2 Forming a Critical Discourse

Although letterpress printing has its own specific history, new work on this subject must, of course, be situated in relation to the broader critical debates about gender in book history. In a 2020 roundtable hosted by the Bibliographical Society of America entitled 'Building Better Book Feminisms', Leslie Howsam looked back at her 1998 article in *SHARP News*, 'In My View: Women and Book History'. In writing that piece, she intended to begin a conversation in the field about the fact that, although book history as a whole tends either to be treated as a genderless, object-oriented space or to default to masculinity, 'women can be identified at every node in the cycle and at all periods in history'.[15] While the work of feminist recovery has highlighted specific women involved in the production of books – from widows managing printing operations after their husband's death to feminist collectives running publication initiatives specifically aimed at female readerships – Howsam noted that the methodological structure of book history could hardly be considered feminist.[16] Reflecting on this piece twenty-two years later, Howsam remarked that she had hoped it would be the first in a great number of feminist book historical ventures and that it would spark a lively conversation in our field.[17] And so she waited . . . and waited. In spite of Howsam's call to bring women's labour and practice more to the fore in book history discussions, Kate Ozment, writing in 2019, persuasively delineates the ways in which 'the history of the book *is still* largely defined as a male homosocial environment where female figures are briefly mentioned on the margins of textual production or invisible altogether'.[18] In spite of the rich tradition of work on women and print on which I build here, there is clearly still more to be done, particularly on the matter of how we theorize gender in book history.

A practice of feminist book history scholarship depends on an explicitly and generously citational ethos that acknowledges lineages of discourse both within and outside the field. As Ozment points out, however, the establishment of canonical and overly rigid critical and methodological approaches can be just as limiting in practice as relying on a small selection of frequently repeated case studies and examples. If we continue to rely too heavily on Robert Darnton's models and examples for book history – which was never his intent in any case in creating them – we risk missing what might exist outside or beyond or even deeper within Darnton's 'communications circuit' and lose some of the sociological structures and nuances that underlie each of the different components of the model itself.[19] Part of the reason for my granular focus in this Element on letterpress printing

---

[15] Howsam, 'In My View', p. 1.   [16] Ibid., pp. 1–2.

[17] Evangelestia-Dougherty et al., 'Building Better Book Feminisms'.

[18] Ozment, 'Rationale for Feminist Bibliography', p. 50 (emphasis added).

[19] Darnton, 'What Is the History of Books?', p. 68.

specifically, and even on a particular kind of letterpress printer, is to isolate a component of book historical production that has its own complex and specific history of gendered labour practices and subsequent artistic refashionings. Part of what I seek to do in this Element is to suggest – as Alice Staveley put it, recontextualizing for book history Gertrude Stein's phrase that there 'is a there there' – that the broader subject of women and letterpress is one we can treat with the same analytical force as we do the purportedly genderless or object-oriented history of print.[20] The metaphor of the constellation might serve us as feminist historians here: we can apprehend patterns and images even as we acknowledge the limited nature of our own perspectives.

The gender dynamics of the book trade at large are, as has been amply documented, more nuanced and diverse than the specific history of women and letterpress.[21] Unlike bookbinding, which has a long, rich history of women's participation;[22] unlike editorial and secretarial work, which was historically (and often invisibly) done by women (particularly as the industry began to be 'feminized' through the nineteenth century, as Sarah Lubelski has shown in her excellent study of Bentley's);[23] unlike the 'feminizing' of typesetting in the photocomposition era, when it could be done at a keyboard;[24] when the physical work of operating a printing press was a foundational part of the commercial trade, women could run the feeding station of a steam press but not actually operate it. J. A. Stein argues that printing and specifically the role of the press machinist continued into the 1980s to call up a specific association with 'masculine craft identities'.[25] Even as offset lithography began to take over in the trade, there was a further retrenchment of gendered roles, including 'a masculine embodiment that was attuned to and shaped by the materiality and aesthetics of printing technologies'.[26] Stein further notes that the

---

[20] Staveley, in conversation, May 2021.

[21] For broader bibliographic work on gender in this scholarly field, see Coker and Ozment's excellent 'Women in Book History Bibliography'.

[22] See Tidcombe, *Women Bookbinders*.

[23] Lubelski, 'A Gentlewoman's Profession'.   [24] See Cockburn, *Brothers*.

[25] Stein, *Hot Metal*, p. 75.   [26] Ibid.

continuation of this gendered dynamic in the print industry after the commercial decline of letterpress points to the fact that these masculine associations were not tied specifically to letterpress traditions but were related to 'other dimensions of technology, such as aesthetics, design, embodied "know-how" and the physical presence of large-scale machinery on the shop floor'.[27] I would like to define and interrogate the gendered resistance culture that arises in letterpress communities of the twentieth century and, particularly with the rise of online communities, into the twenty-first. What does it look like to take a craft with a history of masculine professional identities and make it feminist or feminine or nonbinary? What does it mean, moreover, to make it into a frequently and deliberately amateur undertaking – something you learn not necessarily through a formal apprenticeship or a trade school but through old manuals scavenged from used book sales or borrowed from libraries, from friends in your own little studio, or simply through trial and error?

1.3 Constellated Historiography

Print feminisms, perhaps unsurprisingly, follow the broad strokes of the history of feminism through the twentieth century and into the twenty-first: from the first wave of suffragettes using letterpress to make posters and pamphlets[28] through to the present day of interrogating what narratives of predominantly white women's history can mean for intersectional constructions of gender[29] that unravel hegemonic categories. As the labour structures around women's participation changed through the course of the century, so too did the content of the prints, reflecting the feminisms of the moment.

Part of what I intend to do in this Element is to intervene methodologically in the field by considering how and why we might approach the study of women printers in a constellated rather than a comprehensive fashion. I focus here on some very bright stars and some less visible ones, and some patterns and implications arise from seeing them together, but I make no attempt here to suggest that I'm showing the whole firmament. The figure of the constellation has helped me to think about the extremely

[27] Ibid. [28] See Murray, 'Deeds and Words'. [29] See Mowris, 'What I Learned'.

challenging process of example selection in a time period that is so full, so diverse, and so complex that drawing out particular examples almost inevitably feels either overdetermined by existing canons of print culture or feminist history or else completely random. Thinking about feminist historiography as a constellated practice allows patterns and suggestions of meaning to come into and fall out of view; it suggests that some kind of narrative is possible but that comprehensiveness is not the goal. I also hope to offer a method in which other views of the field are not only possible but explicitly welcome. I hope readers will consider this Element an enthusiastic invitation to future work in this area, particularly in contexts outside Britain and North America.

Rather than providing a comprehensive collection of women who print using letterpress in the twentieth and twenty-first centuries, I instead gather a constellation of examples in order to suggest what it might mean more broadly for the historical masculinities of letterpress printing culture to encounter non-dominant gendered experiences. The inevitable gaps and silences in this Element are due in part to the uneven nature of research on printing history and particularly on the aspects that go beyond the actual printed documents themselves to consider questions of labour and affective experience. In the secondary literature on women and print, noting the fragmentary nature of the archival record is something of a critical commonplace. Dianne L. Roman describes the sources on pre-nineteenth-century American women in print as 'unruly, tangled, and for some, nonexistent'.[30] Roman also points out that even existing well-known resources, such as Lois Rather's *Women As Printers* (1970) are not always consistent or accurate, and materials are often gathered from a variety of sometimes unlikely places and pieced together. Maryam Fanni, Matilda Flodmark, and Sara Kaaman favour the term 'messy history', coined by the graphic designer Martha Schofield, to describe their gathering of historical documents and essays on the history of women in graphic design. They describe their materials as a 'collage of images',[31] another helpful aesthetic figure for thinking about feminist historiography as a citational

---

[30] Roman, 'Detangling the Medusa', p. 83.
[31] Fanni, Flodmark, and Kaaman, *Natural Enemies of Books*, p. 14.

and yet non-comprehensive practice. The challenges of collecting thorough resources have led to a frequent practice, too, of list and bibliography making. In 1983, Barb Wieser of the Iowa City Women's Press compiled a directory of women printers and typesetters but was careful to emphasize that it was 'only a partial listing'.[32] Cait Coker and Kate Ozment's 'Women in Book History Bibliography' and the Alphabettes bibliography of women in type[33] follow similar impulses to collect and continually expand the range of reference for this discipline. The narrative threads in this Element are necessarily and deliberately fragile, in keeping with feminist traditions of form and narration that argue against teleological or developmental historical narratives and in favour of instances of resonance within the historical record that can illuminate their surroundings without overdetermining the story.

Part of the reason for the fragility of these many distributed archives of print history and for the fragmented components of the historical record is that, while it is most often straightforward to find out directly from a printed object or from a library catalogue which publisher or press printed a book, it is much more difficult to be precise about who did the actual printing, and even less straightforward to establish or discern the gender identity of that person. Elis Ing and Lauren Williams are currently investigating the work of women printers in McGill Library's Special Collections, and one of their search techniques has been to look for the words 'veuve' or 'widow'; prior to the twentieth century, it was common for women to have their printing work in family firms acknowledged only after their husbands had died.[34] For the twentieth and twenty-first centuries, such a search would prove less fruitful, since a much wider array of women and non-binary and gender-nonconforming people now engage in printing practices. Since many women were, for reasons I will discuss in Section 2, often not historically

---

[32] Wieser, 'Women's Printshops and Typesetting', p. 9.

[33] Veguillas, 'Women in Type Bibliography'.

[34] Ing and Williams, 'At the Helm but Unheard'. For more on the history of widows as printers, see Moog, 'Women and Widows', and, in the American context, Ford, 'Types and Gender'.

members of official trade unions, sometimes there is very little or no documentation of their employment or their printing output.

The constellation as a spatial figure assumes gaps between luminous points, but those spaces always offer the possibility of future discovery. The printers I do feature here, particularly those in Section 4, connected to a feminist British literary modernist tradition originating with Virginia Woolf, skew affluent, white, literary or artistic, and well-connected. They are some of the people who left substantive documentary evidence of their labour and their process and whose work speaks to one another, and it is worth acknowledging that there were many more women – and, notably, women of colour – working as letterpress printers in this time period. Many will have left very little trace beyond the books they printed, many of which would not have borne even their names.[35] It is partly because of the collaborative nature of textual production that historical evidence of these experiences is difficult to come by: printers don't always (or even often) write about printing, neither do they always (or even often) appear in photographs. As Christine Moog notes, writing about some of the earliest women working in the book trade, 'roles that women in the industry have played have largely been ignored – in part due to lack of archival material and in part due to the fact that when women produced printed pieces, they often either did not attribute their names to their work or instead credited themselves as "heirs of a master printer"'.[36] Writing in 1981 for the journal *Library Review*, the printer Jean Engel urged women's studies scholars to take notice of women printers in spite of the dispersed and sometimes unconventional nature of the materials they were producing: 'We need librarians to be aware of the existence and importance of woman-produced materials, even though they don't fit the norm. We need women's studies faculty to be aware of the publishing and printing origins of the texts they use and of their own options in feminist publishing.'[37] Institutional collections definitely contain women's materials, but it is also crucial in the history of printing more generally to consider alternative spaces that might house

---

[35] For an examination of the available sources in the early American context, see Barlow, *Notes on Woman Printers*.

[36] Moog, 'Women and Widows', p. 3. [37] Engel, 'Why Feminist Printers?', p. 15.

some otherwise uncollected materials. The contemporary poet and printer Lauren Elle DeGaine, writing of her historical work on women type designers, proposes internet auction sites as other important repositories for research:

> The 'eBay archive' allows women's work to be recovered from the margins and provides a piece of the story of the role of women in design, print culture, and book history. Such commercial sites comprise a kind of extra-institutional international finding aid that has become an important scholarly mechanism for recovering research material currently missing from institutional archives. At the same time, it also highlights the instability of material culture traded in the open market.[38]

Engel's call for preservation of textual forms that might not always make it into conventional collections aligns with Alan Galey's work on what he calls 'pro-am' or pro-amateur online archives.[39] Printing historians, particularly those who once worked in the trade, are avid collectors and cataloguers, particularly of historical equipment. These digital spaces are often sites of memory and collection that contain tremendously rich detail unavailable elsewhere. DeGaine's emphasis on seeking out and locating unconventional sources for historical materials shows that part of the way in which we can ensure preservation of these stories is by writing and thinking about them even in the absence of a robust or coherent institutionalized historical record. For research on contemporary letterpress practitioners, web communities, the Instagram archive, and the TikTok archive are particularly vital.[40]

---

[38] DeGaine, 'The "eBay Archive"', para. 15.

[39] See Galey, 'Looking for a Place to Happen'.

[40] I will discuss the online communities of letterpress more in Section 1, but a good example of an online community output is Brown, Detlef, and Townsend, *Proof: A Letterpress Podcast*, in which letterpress practitioners discuss their practices and equipment.

1.4 The Embodied Language of Print

I began with the personal story of my own entry into letterpress printing because, as an embodied cognitive experience, **typesetting** and printing are practices that you need to physically do in order to learn. By undertaking the print process by hand, you learn the language and the nuances of what it means to press type into paper and thereby make an impression. As Sarah Werner argues, there is no escaping gender, even in the seemingly object-oriented world of bibliography: 'If I'm only interested in the mechanics of printing, need I think about gender at all?' Werner asks; 'Well, yes, always yes, but especially yes in Renaissance England, where the word "press" was a term that could be used both to refer to printing but also a physical pressing of a man into a woman, that is, an act of sexual penetration and deflowering.'[41] Wendy Wall points to the 'bawdy' implications of the phrase 'undergo a pressing', which in Elizabethan drama referred to 'act[ing] the lady's part', giving rise to what Wall describes as the many 'contradictions and slippages'[42] inherent in the gendered language of print. The etymological layering of 'press' is just one example of printing terminology as a language of the body. We speak of type 'faces', and the anatomy of a **sort** is itself a gendered one: it has a body, a shoulder, feet, and a beard.[43]

Printing is a discipline rife with puns. The bodily language of typography suggests multiple layers of meaning and interpretation, even if many of the literal origins of printing terms and expressions we now use have become dead metaphors. The affective valences of printing words and phrases often reveal themselves when the terms are reconnected to their printing origins. 'Out of sorts' in printing refers to the heart-stopping moment of setting a job and realizing you haven't enough letters (**sorts**) left in your case to say what you mean; uppercase and lowercase letters have their origins in the spatial positioning of type cases; and 'mind your p's and q's' (that general phrase exhorting people to fastidiousness) is in printing an expression that refers to the easy confusion for printers between these two

[41] Werner, 'Working Towards a Feminist Printing History', p. 6.

[42] Wall, *The Imprint of Gender*, p. 2.

[43] Gaskell, *New Introduction to Bibliography*, p. 9.

sorts. I include a Glossary of printing terminology (indicated in bold) at the end of this Element in part to orient the reader and ensure that the specialist terminology itself is not used in an exclusionary fashion but in part also to foreground myriad ways in which the language of print is multivalent and slips easily into a layered historical discourse.

The matter of printing language also raises aesthetic questions. One specific way of tracing the shift in the nature of letterpress through the twentieth century and into the twenty-first is to follow its shifting material aesthetic. The varying depths of impression that type can make in paper are called '**bite**' (deep) and '**kiss**' (light) impressions. It is impossible not to see the embodied implications of these terms, describing an encounter between paper and type in a language of intimate physical exchange. Letterpress printing that kisses the paper just lightly enough to produce an even impression was, until recently, considered the most skilful and pleasing outcome; this way there was no indent visible on the back of the page, so double-sided printing could occur without obscuring any text.

Other methods of printing, such as digital and **offset** methods, do not produce this bite at all, and so it has become a kind of aesthetic shorthand for a material experience that announces its connections to the past, even though historically printers were trying to be 'kissers' rather than 'biters'. As the printer Amelia Hugill-Fontanel notes, William Morris had an influence in bringing 'bite' impressions into favour among fine printers in the nineteenth century, and ever since 'it's been traditionally understood that the kissers were commercial and the biters were fine printers'.[44] In the twenty-first century, the 'bite' of letterpress is what indicates a certain authenticity, regardless of the type of print being produced. Musing on the modern popularity of the bite impression, the printer and founder of Ladies of Letterpress, Kseniya Thomas, speculates on the possibility of the bite coming into popularity because of the shift towards a more amateur print culture in the twentieth and twenty-first centuries: 'I almost wonder if the deep impression we associate with letterpress today came about when people without printing backgrounds came to letterpress, pulled their first

[44] Hugill-Fontanel, 'Impression', para. 4.

print on their old press, and realized that the default setting – a palpable impression – was beautiful.'[45] The foregrounding and prevalence of bite impressions highlight materiality and emphasize a 'printishness' akin to Jessica Pressman's concept of the distinctly twentieth- and twenty-first-century phenomenon of 'bookishness': 'a creative movement invested in exploring and demonstrating love for the book as symbol, as art form, and as artefact'.[46] Just as bookish artists and enthusiasts delight in leather bindings, the aesthetics of illustrated dust jackets, and the codex as an art medium, printers who foreground the materiality of their practice are deliberately emphasizing the particular sensorial qualities of print.

One complicating issue with the contemporary trend for bite impressions is that to press lead into paper, especially if the paper has not be dampened first, requires the printer to use so much **packing** as to make a deep bite is also to damage the type. Little by little, the **metal type** is worn away by this approach, and older **wood type** can crack under too much pressure. When so much of the type that printers today use is antique and, in some cases irreplaceable, there is concern, especially in the conservation community, that aggressive biting is inappropriately degrading pieces of type as artefacts. Hugill-Fontanel concludes her essay on 'Impression' with this advice to printers: '[D]on't settle into the bite for bite's sake hoopla ... Practice safe impression!'[47] Yet, since the bite is what distinguishes relief from digital printing, it's unlikely that the aesthetic preference for deep impressions will go away any time soon; in fact, many printers have found ways around this by creating new **photopolymer plates** that don't need quite such a careful approach as antique blocks and **sorts** do. The bite offers a tactile experience that contains vestiges of strength and power. One way of distinguishing letterpress or relief printing from laser or digital is to run a finger along the text. The texture resulting from a bite impression matters and has meaning to letterpress printers of the twentieth and twenty-first centuries, who practice this craft even as it is no longer a commercially dominant

---

[45] 'An Interview with Kseniya Thomas', para. 11. [46] Pressman, *Bookishness*, p. 1.
[47] Hugill-Fontanel, para. 10.

printing technology. The kiss is still prized by many practitioners and in library and museum settings, but the biters are also here to stay.

It might be worth pausing here for a moment, speaking of the bite and the kiss, to consider what exactly an **impression** is and what it means to make one. In various contexts, the term takes on new meanings: in elocution or poetic metre, an impression refers to a stress or emphasis; materially, it's a mark produced on any surface by pressure; and even in the specialized discourse of printing and bibliography, there are numerous meanings of the term, since it refers to the mark made by the type in the paper but also to a printing of a number of copies that form one issue or course of printing. Impressions in the social or interpersonal sense are nearly always gendered in myriad conscious and unconscious ways. Like Cathleen A. Baker and Rebecca M. Chung, the editors of *Making Impressions: Women in Printing and Publishing* (2020), I find the layered meaning useful when thinking about women in print: they 'make impressions' in all of these different senses of the word. As sometimes-conspicuous historical outsiders, women stood out in print shops as they pressed their words into paper. Much more broadly, the OED offers a general definition of the noun 'impression' as 'the action involved in the pressure of one thing upon or into the surface of another; also, the effect of this',[48] and an 1875 English translation of Plato's *Dialogues* follows this same sense: '[T]he creation of the world is the impression of order on a previously existing chaos.'[49] As I discuss particularly in relation to the work of Anaïs Nin in Part 3, this sense of seeking solace also applies in a print context: there is something consoling about the 'impression of order', even if that order is available only as a neatly **distributed** and organized typecase.

1.5 Letterpress in the Late Age of Print

While an entirely linear or progressive narrative history of letterpress would involve some oversimplification, it is important to acknowledge the basic technological shift that attends this moment in print history. In their account of the material and technological development of print technologies in the twentieth century, Sarah Bromage and Helen William

---

[48] 'Impression', n., para. 1.   [49] Ibid.

note that 'until the middle of the twentieth century print production remained a labour intensive process. The traditional work practices that had existed since the mid-1800s remained largely unchanged and the work-force was strictly demarcated along work role and gender lines.'[50] What happens to those reified work roles and gender lines when this old technology finds itself decontextualized in a contemporary context? Even as letterpress ceased to be the technology of choice for newspapers, novels, and many other kinds of everyday texts, towards the end of the twentieth century, it gained a new market for upscale commercial ephemeral products, including wedding invitations and business cards.[51] It continued, at the same time, to be a form that suited and was intimately tied to experimental literature, activism, and poetry. The 100 years leading up to our present moment – an era Ted Striphas terms 'the late age of print', – are marked by a 'persistent unevenness' and 'dynamism'[52] in the use of print technologies and in the purposes to which those technologies are put. In the case of letterpress printing, Striphas' characteristic late twentieth- and early twenty-first-century 'dynamism' is embodied in the shift away from commercial and newspaper printing at the start of the century and towards art-making, poetry broadside printing, protest posters, postcards, and wedding invitations at the century's end.

While the vital work of feminist print historians working on earlier periods informs this project, in this study, I am most interested in print production in the twentieth century into the twenty-first, and particularly the relationship between letterpress technologies and experimental literary works created by self-taught modernist women writers. The choice of letterpress when other technologies are available is important but often overlooked in the context of the longer history of the book. Much of the scholarly work on book history and on practices of printing – everything from Robert Darnton's 'What is the History of Books?' (1982, and revisited in 2008) to Roger

---

[50] Bromage and William, 'Materials, Technology, and the Printing Industry', p. 41.

[51] A search for 'letterpress' on the digital handmade craft marketplace, Etsy, as of this writing, turns up over 50,000 results: https://www.etsy.com/ca/search?q=letterpress

[52] Striphas, *The Late Age of Print*, p. ix.

Chartier's 'The Author's Hand to the Printer's Mind' (2013) – specifically focusses on historical periods in which letterpress printing is the dominant commercial mode of transmission for texts. The essential bibliographical and scholarly work of Cait Coker, Margaret J. M. Ezell, Wendy Wall, Helen Smith, Michelle Levy, Kate Ozment, and Sarah Werner, and others on women in print, focusses primarily on a time period when letterpress printing was the default technology for textual circulation. By the mid-twentieth century, however, letterpress printing was no longer something that needed to be done in order for a text or a piece of print to reach its audience. As letterpress printing became more of an aesthetic choice and an artistic practice through the twentieth century, it reverberated with meanings that carried valences inherited from the complicatedly gendered traditions described in earlier periods, often in unpredictable and subtle ways. As the viability of letterpress within the printing industry dwindled with the rise of newer, more efficient equipment, letterpress printing became aligned with museum culture, with heritage, with art, and with community-based and activist initiatives. The histories of feminist do-it-yourself (DIY) initiatives from the beginning of the twentieth century and into the twenty-first are fragmented and often moving. These are stories of resilience and power, and of aesthetic and political radicalism.

1.6 Letterpress as Contemporary Craft

Because letterpress printing and especially hand-setting type became an increasingly niche activity in the twentieth century, it now calls up the full complexity and slipperiness of 'craft' as a concept. Drawing on and extending David Pye's classic formulations of craft theory in *The Nature of Art and Workmanship* (1968), Alexandra Peat argues that in the early twentieth century: '[C]raft could be the authentically human handmade alternative to industrial modernity or something automotive and mechanical; it could be a skilled profession or work done by an amateur with a sense of vocation; it could be the opposite to art or elevated to an art form; it could designate the solidly material or it could carry a spiritual resonance.'[53] Fundamental to Pye's theory of craft is the distinction between what he calls the

---

[53] Peat, 'A Word to Start an Argument', p. 36.

'workmanship of risk' and the 'workmanship of certainty'. In the former, the outcome or product of a craft practice is not predetermined but depends on the execution of a process by a fallible human being, whereas the latter implies the precision and replicability of modern industrial practice. Pye suggests that printing occupies a complex position between these two poles, requiring skill and care but also resulting in duplication of a similar result over and over once the type is ready to print (one element of risk he leaves out, I think, which I will return to in Part 3 in my discussion of Virginia Woolf's printing practice, is the contingency of inking). Pye's association of print with certainty is also an indication of the complex status of print and its relation to the notion of making by hand. Walter Benjamin famously aligns print with reproducibility and replication that lacks 'the here and now of the original'.[54] And yet printing using **hand presses** with **movable type** now seems difficult to dissociate from traditions of craft and the handmade when the alternative of digital printing is even further removed from the originating hand and far more 'certain' in the prints' easy sameness. Pye argues in his work that in an era when industrial production suffused with certainty is available, craft that involves risk and a great deal of skill and time must be undertaken 'for love and not for money'.[55] His theory prefigures also a shift in critical discursive practices in the later part of the twentieth century towards thinking about craft practice as closely aligned with particular forms of contemporary art.

Glenn Adamson points to the specific and complex character of craft practice in the modern and contemporary eras and suggests that 'modern craft would be best seen not as a paradox or an anachronism, or a set of symptoms, but as a means of articulation. It is not a way of thinking outside of modernity, but a modern way of thinking otherwise.'[56] The contradictory and slippery nature of craft and its implications are essential in considering the specific nature of letterpress as a creative and material practice. Betty Bright describes contemporary letterpress practice as one experiencing a historic shift in materials, making it 'a medium ripe for

---

[54] Benjamin, 'The Work of Art in the Age of Mechanical Reproducibility', p. 21.

[55] Pye, 'The Nature of Art and Workmanship', p. 349.

[56] Adamson, 'Introduction', p. 5.

artistic restatement'.[57] That restatement, however, has occurred variously and with a great deal of complexity. Bright describes the contemporary landscape as one in 'a state of healthy confusion, as we seek a paradigm that links craft with art and yet is flexible enough to absorb new practices without shutting out the accumulated knowledge that is their backstory'.[58] This paradigm involves an incredibly delicate balancing act: managing to encourage the lineages and histories of craft practices while at the same time opening up to innovation in what can be an incredibly particular and precise practice with very specific standards and rules. As Peat notes, the reputation of craft often splits dichotomously in a divided critical landscape, but letterpress printing seems to hold all of these contradictions within it: printing by hand is often an 'and' rather than an 'or' – art and its opposite, amateur and professional, spiritual and solidly material. Craft – like form, as I discussed earlier – is a concept that not only crosses but disassembles the boundaries between material and linguistic: now a contentiously debated term in creative writing pedagogy, the craft of language and the craft of print overlay in uncertain and often ambivalent relation.[59]

Another 'and' that applies to certain kinds of modern handicraft is that it's often part of both the past and present. Through the twentieth century and into the twenty-first, therefore, letterpress printing undergoes a transformation from a dominant professional technology essential to the circulation of texts to a niche historically informed pursuit. For modernist and mid-century writers, the use of this technology complicates the very modernity of the works being produced by hand and introduces the rich and manifold questions of craft and aesthetics that come with the choice of hand-printing over mechanical or digital process that are more efficient on a commercial scale.

1.7 Why Letterpress?

A question that must be applied to any examination letterpress of our current era is *why* do this difficult, finicky, time-consuming thing now, in

---

[57] Bright, 'Handwork and Hybrids', p. 135.　[58] Ibid., p. 149.

[59] For nuanced perspectives on creative writing education and the discourse of craft, see Salesses, *Craft in the Real World* and Wesbrook et al., *Beyond Craft*.

the twent-first century, when other options for making words appear on paper or even on screens are readily available? The contemporary jeweler and writer Bruce Metcalf asks a similar question of handcraft more generally: 'Why bother when cutting-edge technology is moving towards the complete automation of manufacturing? ... Isn't it stupidly nostalgic and obsolete, or nearly so?'[60] Metcalf points to psychologist Mihaly Csikszentmihalyi's concept of 'flow' – a state of deep concentration in which a practitioner feels transported to a realm of intense enjoyment that rewards the hard and patient work, and that often goes into highly skilled activities – as a motivator for craft practitioners. As the printers Cathie Ruggie Saunders and Martha Chiplis point out, there is a strong affective pull for those interested in letterpress now: '[T]here is little pleasure greater than the satisfaction gleaned from the humble punch of metal into paper.'[61] The printing historian Will Ransom similarly suggested in 1929 that maybe the best reason to print is for the pleasure of printing: 'The simplest and perhaps truest type of private press is that maintained by one who is, at least by desire, a craftsman and finds particular joy in handling type, ink, and paper, with sufficient means and leisure to warrant such an avocation. His literary selection may leave something to be desired and art may be disregarded or amazingly interpreted, but he has a good time.'[62] Ransom's observation here – with its male pronouns, characteristic for the time – is also indicative of a longstanding rift between book art as material art and as literary content. Print quality and verse quality were not always aligned, and this notion that book arts and literary arts can operate independently of one another is one reason it remains challenging to marry the two. Learning how to print and learning how to write require very different modes and kinds of education in two historically separate disciplines. It's important to note also in Ransom's suggestion the privileged nature of this craft, especially when it's undertaken as an amateur pursuit rather than as a profession: in 1929 as now, it requires 'sufficient means and leisure' to produce letterpress prints, particularly if the press is not a specifically or dominantly commercial enterprise.

---

[60] Metcalf, 'The Hand', para. 5. [61] Saunders and Chiplis *For the Love*, p. 11.
[62] Ransom, 'What Is a Private Press?', p. 118.

The possible justifications for producing letterpress works also change through the course of the twentieth century. At first, small hand presses and other such printing equipment was being sold off from the trades and was relatively readily available; buying a tabletop Kelsey or Adana press in 1930 might be something like buying a photocopier/scanner today (Anaïs Nin, about whom I write more later, bought her treadle-operated platen press for $75 USD in 1941, which is the equivalent of about $1,250 USD in 2021 currency. Similarly, the woodcut artist J. J. Lankes purchased a Washington-Hoe press for $50,[63] 'shortly after the war when [he] was given to understand that many were broken up and disposed of as scrap iron – no doubt for making shells, a more profitable business than making prints)'.[64] In 1929, the Excelsior Printing Supply Company was advertising its small tabletop Kelsey 3'x5' presses along with a starter kit of supplies and an instructional manual for $15.70 USD.[65]

For printers working for much of the century, the choice of letterpress as a technology was less about historical nostalgia and more about agency and availability: the larger commercial presses were dauntingly large and heavy, and digital printing obviously wasn't available until relatively recently. To make beautiful prints within a domestic setting, a tabletop hand press like a Kelsey (in the United States) or an Adana (in the UK) was a logical choice. In the twenty-first century, however, and as a resurgence in demand for these smaller presses also started to arise, the availability of the machines decreased and the cost correspondingly increased. Now, various do-it-yourself and even build-it-yourself printing presses have been devised both for sale and for wider distribution. The Provisional Press Project, for example, arose during the 2020 pandemic as a means of distributing functional flat-bed platen presses for artists and students who lacked access to their studios during public health closures.[66] The prevalence of these kinds of new technology for an old craft brings us back to the relief

---

[63] Approximately $740 USD in 2021. [64] Lankes, *A Woodcut Manual*, p. 26.

[65] Approximately $250.00 USD in 2021. For more on the history of Kelsey, including several digitized advertisements, see Alan Runsfeld's resource 'The Excelsior Press Museum Print Shop'.

[66] 'Provisional Press', para. 1.

impression as a primary motivation for letterpress printing: without the cast-iron originals creating the prints, the bite impression itself is the remaining element that links a letterpress work back to print history.

It is important to note that obsolescence isn't quite the right way of describing letterpress, even today, because the old machinery – assuming it's been cared for or restored –actually still works, and in many ways the hybrid practices of digital technology and letterpress become more and more effective at printing as the century goes on. This is not the experience of trying to run Windows 95 on a 2020 PC, in which case the operating system is obsolete in the sense that it no longer functions in concert with a new machine. This is rather more like the contemporary trend, indicated by the popularity of social media and crafting sites like Ravelry and Etsy, for knitting. The knitting needles still work as knitting needles have done since eleventh-century Egypt – it is just that there is no need to use them these days in order to procure a garment to help you stay warm. The time and embodied consciousness that made a piece of letterpress printing is there, even if, or maybe especially because, you can't always see it and even if, or perhaps especially because, you could get the words on the page more expediently in some other way.

2 Learning

This part explores the question of how letterpress printing, as a skilled craft, has been taught and learned through the twentieth century and into the twenty-first. Throughout this section, I show how printers' educations and labour conditions have been gendered. A crucial thread here is the contrast between education in formal trades and union participation and education that occurs outside those structures through books, online resources, and manuals, or through small print networks or countercultural groups. This distinction in modes of education and degrees of labour organization also raises the matter of distinguishing between fine printers, in the tradition of, for instance, William Morris's Kelmscott Press, and focussing on newspapers, advertisements, handbills, and other trade content.

I hope that in addition to outlining the history of how different kinds of printers learned to print, this section might also be fruitfully used as a resource for teaching, especially in combination with some of the supplementary materials in the bibliography. I therefore begin here with my own brief illustration of the basic process of setting type and printing by hand. I then move through the historical structures and debates around printing education and labour organization through the century. This part lays the foundation for understanding and interpreting the written accounts, images, and prints in the sections that follow: in order to appreciate the significance of printing language, it's important to understand the mechanics of the process and how these mechanics reflected the complex characterization of printing as a form of craft, a form of art, and a form of labour.

2.1 Fundamentals of the Letterpress Printing Process

When people are learning to set type, what exactly is it that they need to know? The metaphors and figural connections that writers and printers ascribe to the language of their medium is governed by a very specific set of material acts, objects, and principles. To begin from the (mechanical) beginning: letterpress is a form of relief printing in which an inked, raised surface is impressed on a piece of paper or other substrate. Before 1900, it wouldn't have been particularly necessary to put the 'letterpress' in front of 'printing', because textual printing would almost always have been done this

Figure 2 The process of setting type and printing on an Adana tabletop press. Photograph by and of the author, 2014.

way.[67] The machine used to create this type of print varied over time and still varies, and the degree of handwork required can be more or less depending on the intervening technologies that aid the process.

For the most basic letterpress setup, **composing** (sometimes otherwise called setting type, hand setting, or typesetting) takes place letter by letter, with individual sorts lined up in a **composing stick**.

Each line is then placed on a large, flat **imposing stone** and surrounded with wooden **furniture**, locked up using metal **quoins** into a frame called a **chase**, and then the whole thing – now called a **forme** – is laid on the **press bed**. The whole process of preparing for printing is called **makeready**. Then, **ink** is applied either directly to the type on the form using a **hand roller** or using an automatic inking function on the machine. The substrate is fed into the machine – and there are many variations on possible types of machine, ranging from the portable **tabletop press** to behemoth poster presses, which I will discuss further later – and then, voilà!, you can **pull**

[67] Many excellent general histories of printing are available. For the classic bibliographical starting point, see Gaskell, *A New Introduction to Bibliography*.

your print. In many larger commercial operations, the **compositor** who set the type and the **pressman** who pulled the prints were separate roles carried out by individuals with distinct skills and training, although learning the whole trade was often part of an apprenticeship process, and in many small operations a printer would carry out all the roles.

Linotype and **intertype** machines, invented in the late nineteenth and early twentieth centuries, and used widely until the 1970s and 1980s, mechanized the typesetting process. The operator used a keyboard to assemble **matrices**, not sorts, which then cast a whole line at a time (a 'line o' type' also called a **slug**) and eliminated one step in the process of typesetting. In the UK, **monotype**, a different process using perforated paper tape, was the preferred technological advancement in typesetting. These machines eliminated the need to hold a stick of type and the labour of **dissing** it for reuse after printing. Once the work was printed, used slugs could be melted down to be reused, and the process began over again. Commonly used early in the century in newspaper operations, linotype casters were huge and expensive, so they tended not to be common in domestic or small operations. However, there are still a few of them kicking around in operation at small presses today.[68] Later in the twentieth century, it became hard even to give them away, and many were scrapped after they fell out of general use for newspapers in the 1980s. The preservation, restoration, and resale of letterpress equipment has become a highly specialized, niche activity. It is now possible to acquire some equipment through eBay and other online marketplaces, as DeGaine reminds us, but for much of the later twentieth century and early twenty-first, specialist dealers, like Don Black Linecasting in Toronto (now sadly closed) tended to be the most reliable providers to furnish new printers with equipment that had been lovingly restored to usable condition.

2.2 Hierarchies of Labour: Apprenticeships, Unions, and the Printing Trade

Before considering the twentieth and twenty-first centuries, it's necessary to briefly address the long history of gendered labour in the printing industry

[68] For discussion of the practices of Coach House Press, including a combination of linotype and digital methods, see Maxwell, 'Coach House Press'.

and delineate the ways in which the systems and structures of labour in these worlds continued throughout the century to bear on perceptions of women as printers. Well into the twentieth and twenty-first centuries, the printing industry continued to be impacted by what it inherited: exclusionary trade unions, factory acts that legislated restrictions on female participation in industrial labour, and cultures of misogyny and gender essentialism.

From the fifteenth century onwards, letterpress printing was a trade most commonly learned 'on the job' through a hierarchical apprenticeship programme. Printers' **'devils'**, as they were commonly called, were charged with the dirtiest and most repetitive jobs in the shop: cleaning the floors and dealing with the **'hellbox'** of discarded type destined to go back to the type foundry. Eventually they worked their way up to more skilled roles, but only after having spent years observing the craft and learning from within the printing space. By the nineteenth century, a fairly rigid apprenticeship system of hiring young boys for these jobs was standard across most of Europe. The completion of an apprenticeship led to the status of **journeyman printer**, and as Cynthia Cockburn notes: '[T]he butterfly that emerged from the chrysalis of apprenticeship could never again be confused with the mere grubs of the labouring world';[69] this repeated trope of 'youthful suffering to win manly status' was a significant narrative element of the structure of print education right up to the twentieth century.

It's important to emphasize that the culture of exclusionary and misogynist practice in the print shop did not mean that there were no women printers. It did mean, however, that if women were working in these contexts, no matter the job they were doing, they very rarely had access to the same rigorous training programme as men who performed the same operations. As the historian Ulla Wikander notes, in the nineteenth century: '[G]irls were not accepted into apprenticeship programs. Refusing women access to education was a method of exclusion.'[70] While men could be assured of their professional status in a skilled trade following their apprenticeships, there was, as Sian Reynolds puts it, 'no such thing as a "time-served journeywoman" in printing',[71] even though women did in fact work in the industry. As Mary

[69] Cockburn, *Brothers*, p. 16. [70] Wikander, 'The Battle', p. 107.
[71] Reynolds, *Britannica's Typesetters*, p. 137.

Biggs points out, two basic views of the gender dynamics of the print industry of this early part of the century tend to dominate: '[T]he union view of the typographers as pioneer egalitarians, and the feminist view of the union as a destroyer of the first and best opportunity women had to participate in a remunerative skilled trade. As far as they go, both views are correct.'[72] As in many labour markets, significant political and social complexity arose around the matters of equal pay, training, and unionization, especially since printing was considered a prestigious industrial craft associated with the dissemination of literature and of knowledge. Moreover, as Christina Burr notes: '[A] gender division of labour was in place with women occupying those positions socially defined as unskilled, namely press feeding, and folding, collating, and stitching in the bindery.'[73] These activities notably tended to exclude what is sometimes referred to in contemporary documents as the 'heavy' work of actually pulling the prints: of making impressions. As Karen Holmberg points out, the legacy of assigning women less 'skilled' roles fed back into some of the erasures of labour in the historical record that now pose challenges for historical research: '[E]ven in the latter part of the twentieth century, printing still bore the mark of the masculine-guild mentality; the male was the owner and master printer, while those who labored at setting type, folding, sewing, or binding, were never acknowledged in the published book.'[74]

The recovery of particular settings or stories where women participated in the print industry makes up the bulk of existing secondary criticism about women in print. As Moog notes, one of the earliest and most frequently cited examples of European women printing were the nuns working at the Convent of San Jacopo di Ripoli in Florence in 1476, their labour documented in the convent's records.[75] Women were not always entirely excluded from the labour unions later, either. The International Typographical Union (ITU), founded in the United States of America in 1852, admitted some women as

---

[72] Biggs, 'Neither Printer's Wife Nor Widow,' p. 432.

[73] Burr, 'Defending the Art Preservative', p. 48.

[74] Holmberg, 'Case Studies', p. 200. Holmberg links this phenomenon more broadly in letterpress printing with the artistic 'handmaiden' syndrome described by Olson in *Silences*.

[75] Moog, 'Women and Widows', p. 2.

early as 1869. Women's branches and subgroups and advisory committees arose in various contexts in the nineteenth and early twentieth centuries, including local branches, such as the Women's Co-Operative Printing Union of San Francisco (1869) and the Women's International Auxiliary (1909). Biggs also points to the existence of women-run and operated full production organizations in the nineteenth century, such as the Bohemian Women's Publishing Company of Chicago and the Victoria Press.[76] However, there remained significant complexity and variety in women's participation both in the unions (which also fragmented along different professional lines over the years) and in the industry as a whole, in different national contexts. In France, for example, there was a massive growth in female employment in the printing trades between 1866 and 1896, largely because women were working for less pay and were therefore attractive to employers.[77] The situation was not the same in the UK. There, male union leaders were more successful in excluding women from the trade, and as Reynolds points out, there were further regional differences between the north and the south of the UK and in Scotland. Moreover, the Factory Act of 1867 legislated restrictions on the labour of women in industrial sectors in England: they could work no more than ten hours a day. No such restrictions were placed on men's working hours. As Reynolds notes, in the twentieth century, 'the printing trade was in many countries a particular focus both for new technology and the employment of women'[78] and as such contemporary assessments of the printing trade were sites of debate about female labour in general.

Exclusionary tactics were linguistic as well as practice based. As Alice Staveley remarks, even as women were admitted into unions and were undertaking printing work, 'the rhetoric of exclusion remained powerful and carried a frisson of ecclesiastical prohibition'[79] since the union branches, called '**chapels**', were often possessed of extravagantly masculine cultures. A glaring example of such rhetoric in the printing trades appears in a 1904 study supported by the Women's Industrial Council in the UK called *Women in the Printing Trades: A Sociological Study*. In this work, author J. Ramsay

---

[76] On the latter, see Cait Coker. [77] Wikander, 'The Battle', p. 108.

[78] Reynolds, *Britannica's Typesetters*, p. 6.

[79] Staveley 'My Compositor's Work', p.1.

McDonald (who was subsequently British Prime Minister from 1929 to 1931) lays out the conditions and structures around women's labour and particularly focusses on the matter of equal pay for equal work. In an introductory section, 'The Trades Described', McDonald notes that each step in the letterpress printing process requires 'a high degree of skill and experience ... which women seldom attain'.[80] *Women in the Printing Trades* maintains throughout that it is impossible to see women's work in printing as equal to men's. McDonald suggests that women fail to sufficiently advocate for their own proper conditions of labour and show little ambition for innovation or change: '[S]he has preferred to remain incompetent.'[81] The 'industrial mind and capacity of women'[82] is shown here not to be held in very high regard. Predictable discriminatory ideas about marriage and motherhood as barriers to proper work ('liabilit[ies]'[83] in McDonald's terms), along with a supposed lack of physical strength, fed into an overall dismissal of the notion that women might be considered on any kind of equal ground. Not to mention McDonald's basic understanding of gender itself as fixed, tied to physiology and biological determinism, and devoid of personal or cultural expressions or of a spectrum of possible identities. McDonald's ideas about women printers seem to be shared by the shop and press owners he studies and interviews. One London firm interviewed in the study described the idea of paying women at the same rate as men as 'ridiculous ... They would never be worth as much because they stay so little time.'[84]

Ramsay's study did, however, encourage some feminist discursive interventions into debates about industrialism and labour. Reviewing McDonald's study in the *Journal of Political Economy* in 1905, Edith Abbott writes: '[O]ne is forced to the conclusion that [the causes of inequality outlined by McDonald] are likely to disappear wholly when we have that longed-for "readjustment of traditional modes of thought" to the employment of women; and, with this change in the attitude of the community toward her work, the woman wage-earner will be found to be as energetic, ambitious, and competent as the man.'[85] This first-wave feminist perspective clearly

---

[80] *Women in the Printing Trades*, p. 3.   [81] Ibid., p. 65.   [82] Ibid., p. xvii.

[83] Ibid., p. 66.   [84] Ibid., p. 148.

[85] Abbott, 'Women in the Printing Trades: Book Review', p. 300.

indicates the relationship between discussion of industrial work in the printing industry and perceptions of female labour and gender roles more broadly. Abbott also suggests here that all perceived barriers to women's participation were just that: perceived rather than actual, products of culture rather than empirical facts.

Much later than McDonald's study, there continued to be a male-dominated culture in the industrial world of letterpress printing and particularly in the unions. The union activist and printer Gail Cartmail notes that, in the 1970s and 1980s, the National Graphical Association (NGA) in the UK was jokingly referred to as 'No Girls Allowed'.[86] Reynolds notes that following her own education in hand setting at art college, she learned of the ban on women from joining the NGA, the injustice of which was partly what drove her to write historically about the female compositors who worked on the *Encyclopedia Britannica*.[87] The exclusionary union organization was not a deterrent for Cartmail, who pursued equal pay for women and advocated for a broader diversity in the industry: '[W]hat I know', she writes, 'is that diversity strengthens organizations, and that includes workers' organizations . . . women made it possible for the union to encourage a much wider diversity including ethnicity and understanding aspects of disability.'[88] With Cartmail's remarks, it is possible to trace the emergence of some understanding of intersectional constructions of identity in the world of printing, with its long-standing history of privileging white, male, cis individuals as labouring bodies.

The labour landscape in the commercial world of print altered significantly as new technologies supplanted letterpress as the dominant commercial mode. As letterpress declined in the mid-twentieth century, an alternative method of printing was starting to take over in the commercial trades: **offset lithography.** The key aesthetic difference between lithography and letterpress is that the former is a flat method rather than a relief method. Lithography also differs functionally from letterpress in the sense that the same printing surface can incorporate both text and images, making their

---

[86] Fanni et al., 'Excerpt from a Conversation', p. 151.

[87] Reynolds, *Britannica's Typesetters*, p. 6.

[88] Fanni et al., 'Excerpt from a Conversation', p. 151.

integration on the page much more straightforward. Offset lithography (sometimes called photolithography) really took off in the 1960s. Xerography, the precursor of digital printing, was around by 1949. Technologies coexisted for quite some time, until eventually relief printing became a rarity in the commercial sphere around the mid-to-late 1980s.

By 1986, the ITU had disbanded, owing to the technological shifts that had drastically changed and fragmented the industry. This event in the history of letterpress printing was structurally significant. With the closure of commercial letterpress operations and the move to speedier technologies, the rigid labour structures that had dominated the commercial industry gave way to a more fragmented and less regulated world for letterpress printers. This is the moment – if there can be a single moment – when letterpress structurally moved from industrial practice to craft, and from a highly regulated industry to a world of freelancers, artists, and self-employed practitioners. Cockburn documents this moment of transition in the UK context in her beautiful study *Brothers*, in which she articulates the decline of the compositors' professional role in the 1980s as a transition with an enormous impact on professional cultures of masculinity.

While the dissolution of many of the systems and structures that long governed the industrial print industry made way for more diverse participation, it has also led to a problem now common across industries of late-capitalist neoliberal work structures. Many letterpress printers and graphic designers now work as freelancers or run their own businesses. This of course means they often work without the benefits, standards, and protections afforded to unionized workers. As Fanni, Flodmark, and Kaaman note, the contemporary labour situation is a 'precarious, tough, and in many ways lonely condition. But at the same time framed with apparently positive words like freedom and flexibility'. While the unions had their glaring problems, they also did the important work that unions do of advocating for reasonable conditions, survivable hours, and safe labour practices. They also created communities around the industry, and while they were not communities with open doors or feminist ethics, they offered the possibility of collegiality and shared work. As Fanni, Flodmark, and Kaamen note, their own interest in the history of their professions was sparked by a desire to seek in the past a sense of 'collectivity, community, and an understanding of material conditions'[89] that seems absent in twenty-first-century fragmented and individualistic work conditions.

2.3 Other Ways to Learn: Handbooks and Guides

Since the structures outlined earlier were hardly inclusive, although efforts on the part of women like Cartmail made significant changes, women often learned to print from books and manuals or informally from friends with experience rather than from formal education in schools or from the predictable and rigid systems of trade apprenticeship programmes. The exclusionary structures of printing described also apply most to the commercial trades producing newspapers, large-run bestsellers, and other commercial artefacts.

Smaller operations often took different approaches to education. The poet Laura Riding, for example, learned how to set type from a friend, Vyvyan Richards, who herself had acquired a press to produce fine editions of T. E. Lawrence's work.[90] Virginia Woolf took a similar approach, learning from 'the old printer', Mr McDermott, a neighbour in Richmond, after being denied entry to the London School of Printing because of her class background and her established reputation as a literary journalist. Anaïs Nin learned to print from manuals she borrowed from the library. Yet letterpress printing (especially the part of the process known as **makeready**) is the kind of thing that is much, much easier to learn by being shown physically how to do it. The apprenticeship model in the printing trades was in place for good pedagogical reasons.[91] Even early printing manuals were mostly designed more as notes and reminders for those who had already apprenticed. Learning to print from a printing manual is about as easy as learning to ride a bicycle by

---

[89] Fanni et al., 'Introduction', p. 6.

[90] Borjel, 'The Vampire and the Darling Priest', p. 63.

[91] Even one of the earliest documents of letterpress instruction, Moxon's *Mechanick Exercises* (1685), points to the challenge of describing a physical process in words: 'I thought to have given these *Exercises* the Title of *The Doctrine of Handy-Crafts*; but when I better considered the true meaning of the Word *Handy-Crafts*, I found that *Doctrine* would not bear it; because *Hand-Craft* signifies *Cunning*, or *Sleight*, or *Craft* of the Hand, which cannot be taught by Words, but is only gained by *Practice* and *Exercise*', p. 12.

reading a book about spokes and tires: it is possible, and the guides are definitely useful, but there are better ways.

That said, various manuals and guides to printing were produced from the very earliest days of print, and adapted to reflect the different types of machinery that became available through the century. Manuals were not originally designed as stand-alone resources, but rather as resources for printers who had already undertaken apprenticeships to remind them of good habits and best practices. In her study of some of the most well-known early printing manuals, Joseph Moxon's *Mechanick Exercises* (1685) and John Smith's *The Printer's Grammar* (1755), Maruca points out that while these guides have tended to be read as neutral instructional documents, 'we can begin to glean the local and historical meanings of print [from analyzing manuals] and see it not as a fixed essence, but an active and ever-changing ideological tool.'[92] Reading Moxon's language of typography for its gendered implications, Maruca points to Moxon's 'intense, almost lascivious' descriptions of typecasting as evidence for the frequent linguistic slippage between the bodies of the type and the body of the printing labourer.[93] While the twentieth-century guides are slightly less overtly sexualized than the examples Maruca pulls from Moxon, they nevertheless display a situated gendered identity. A number of pamphlet-sized guides aimed at the hobbyist were included alongside presses when they were purchased, as in this example of *The Printer's Guide Book* produced by the Excelsior company to accompany its hobby-grade tabletop Kelsey presses, complete with an illustration of a well-to-do gentleman in a bowtie with his tabletop press, demurely smoking a pipe as he holds up his perfect print (Figure 3).

From the outset, then, it is clear that even fairly straightforward-seeming technical manuals outlining print processes are far from genderless objects. The manual goes on to show in simple line illustrations and sparse text that 'printing is no mysterious business',[94] although they concede that it does take practice to get good results. To start with, they illustrate the process of setting type and pulling prints, as depicted in Figure 4, starting with the printer's name.

---

[92] Maruca, 'Bodies of Type', p. 323. [93] Ibid., p. 328.
[94] 'The Printer's Guide Book', p. 1.

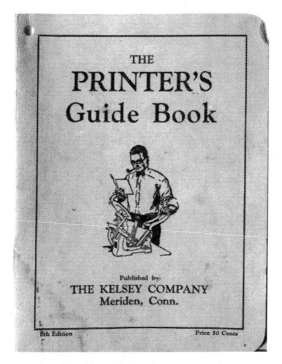

Figure 3 *The Printer's Guide Book* (1929).

In addition to manuals like these that accompanied the presses them-selves, the companies also often produced newsletters with tips and tricks for printers, such as Kelsey's 'The Printer's Helper' and Adana's 'Printswift'. When I examined copies of these I found, unsurprisingly, that the male pronoun was used exclusively in the instructions in these publications. I won't belabour the point, but a characteristic example from a 1963 issue of 'The Printer's Helper' will perhaps suffice to illustrate the tone: 'Every printer knows the necessity of getting all the **lines** in a job of equal tightness if he is not to have trouble with the characters either working up when he is printing or even dropping out before he is able to

HERE'S HOW YOUR PRESS WORKS

These pictures show the main points of printing. The Guide is written so that if you follow it, one step at a time, you can do good printing. However, if you just can't wait, you can

First set your line of type in a composing stick, like this

[or in your chase]

(*Printers hold type as shown on page 6, but the first time hold it this way, if you like.*)

put it in the chase [frame]

open a package of type (see page 4), put it in a case, and set up your name (as shown here). Place it in the chase (frame), also as per picture, put a dab of ink (no bigger than a good sized match head) on the ink table, smooth it out with one of the press rollers, and then take an impression on a piece of paper, turning up the screws on the back of the platen (see page 12) if necessary to make the printing show. The results this way may need considerable improvement,

but they will show you that printing is no mysterious business.

insert a sheet of paper,

You can then go back to the beginning of this Guide, do your next job

push down handle

more slowly, and get first-class, professional results. *Read pages 1 to 11*

for exact details,

see directions in this book.

very carefully. What you find there are the essentials. Beyond page ten

Figure 4 Process illustration from *The Printer's Guide Book* (1929).

get the **chase** in the press. Many learn this through experience, in fact most of us.'[95] The universal 'every printer' gives way here to 'he' the printer, and concludes with the first-person plural: a rhetorical indication that women are not the target audience. While it would be reasonable to argue that the singular 'he' was often used as neutral at this time, the assumed masculinity of the reading audience is even more overt elsewhere in the newsletters. A regular column in the newsletters was the 'A Kelsey Man Comments On' section. The readers who wrote to the newsletter and had their letters printed were men, and there was a general development of a community of 'Kelsey Men' as a kind of brand-identified group. Unlike the large, expensive commercial cylinder presses, the Kelsey tabletop hand presses were generally aimed at amateur printers or at non-printing businesses seeking to do their own printing 'in-house', and even when attempting to sell products to younger users, the target demographic was 'boys' rather than youth or children in general.[96] While the dapper, leisurely masculinity portrayed in these marketing and instructional materials is particular to Kelsey's brand, it indicates that even when access to hobby materials or machines opens up to amateurs outside of the trade, the discourse doesn't cease to be exclusionary. Even if a woman or non-binary person could certainly buy their own Kelsey press to do 'real printing', the accompanying ephemera is evidently not written for her or for them.

The existence of word-of-mouth culture, small collectives, and pamphlets and books for education hasn't, of course, entirely supplanted more formal educational processes for learning how to print. Many women now learn, as I did, to print at university; in studios offering classes; in specialized courses such as the Rare Book School;[97] or in art school. By an informal count there are now at least twenty-six post-secondary printmaking programmes at universities and fine arts schools in the United States of America, the UK, and Canada with dedicated letterpress components.[98] These tend to be part of BFA programmes or graduate arts and humanities programmes, although the variety of courses and offerings

---

[95] 'The Printer's Helper', p. 1.   [96] 'Kelsey Advertisement', p. 1.
[97] 'Rare Book School'.
[98] With thanks to Jess Lanziner for gathering information about these programmes.

crosses disciplines and schools. Even more weekend or week-long work-shops and informal courses through community letterpress studios, museums, and special collections are rising worldwide, and printing museums around the world offer demonstrations, open days, and events.[99]

Online and scholarly communities, too, have generated robust educational resources for learning about craft and technique. The Ladies of Letterpress collective was founded specifically to provide support and training in the absence of industrial apprenticeship: '[I]t's in the context of there being zero formal, long-term training available to would-be printers, and the community of letterpress printers being pretty dispersed, that we started Ladies of Letterpress. This was in 2008, just as it became really easy to start communities of shared affinities online. We set out to fill the gap between enthusiasm and education, and make it easier for people starting out in letterpress to get where they wanted to be.'[100] The open-access resource Letterpress Commons, hosted by Boxcar Press, is a user-generated community that hosts instructional essays, PDFs of manuals for particular machines, a map of letterpress studios around the world, and tips and suggestions for finding internships and other experience.[101] Developed in 2012, the site was designed to provide 'an up-to-date manual of letterpress printing ... one with the capabilities to expand along with the letterpress community'.[102] The Alphabettes collective, which focusses specifically on women in typography and type design, similarly hosts online forums for discussing technique, historical equipment, and other practical matters for letterpress printers, and has cultivated a user community engaged in sharing and disseminating knowledge. The LetPress listserv, Briar Press, Starshaped Press's 'Weekend Printer' blog, the Proof Letterpress Podcast, 'Hamilton Hangs' hosted by Hamilton Wood Type, and the Five Roses Press resource are further examples of online communities that preserve and disseminate practical knowledge for new printers while maintaining and supporting a community of long-time practitioners. The Book/Print Artist/Scholar of Color Collective, founded by Tia Blassingame in 2019, brings together

[99] For a global directory of printing museums, see 'Letterpress: Printing Museums'.

[100] 'An Interview with Kseniya Thomas', para. 13.   [101] 'Letterpress Commons'.

[102] Ibid., para. 1.

and showcases the work and thinking of book artists of color in virtual and live events and collaborative initiatives.[103] These open-access resources serve at once to aggregate resources, while also providing new and experienced printers alike with a community of expertise and knowledge sharing that brings letterpress techniques into the digital age.

[103] Blassingame, 'Book/Print Artist/Scholar of Color Collective'.

3 Individualizing

In this section, I offer biographical vignettes of a small collection of women whose work has shaped the history of twentieth-century women's print culture. The cases I briefly analyze here span the century and range from iconic accounts and depictions of women printing (such as those of Nancy Cunard and Jane Grabhorn) to more obscure examples (such as the pseudonymous local newspaper printer 'Eve', and the nuns of a Montreal convent). Some of these printers' projects aligned with artistic movements such as surrealism, while others fall more into the history of industrial labour in the twentieth century. Through some remaining photographs, it is possible to see female bodies engaged in printing, which presents them both as revived subjects of historical inquiry and in pursuit of their own professional aspirations. Where possible I have reproduced the images here, and elsewhere I have pointed to digital collections and resources that house supplementary visual materials. The wide variety of postures, poses, and compositional strategies depicted in these women's engagement with the machines and materials of printing allows us to see the eclectic mixture of settings, styles, and approaches that women undertook through this period of time. This section's set of biographical and photographic impressions can also help reconceive the gendered history of print: fewer images of and stories about large groups of men in factory settings, more of women undertaking the full process of print production themselves.

3.1 Magique Circonstancielle: Surrealism's Veiled Meanings

One of the most striking sets of images of a woman with a printing press is not in fact of a letterpress process but rather an etching press. The series of photographs taken by the surrealist artist Man Ray of his then-assistant, the artist Meret Oppenheim, in the atelier of the engraver and painter Louis Marcoussis. This sequence was taken in 1933. Man Ray's photographs of Oppenheim offer some of the most powerful commentaries on the layered and complex relations between female bodies, artistic production, and aesthetics. The very presence of nudity alongside industrial equipment immediately destabilizes viewer expectations, and Oppenheim's ironically melodramatic pose against the press calls up a complex series of gendered associations.

Figure 5 Erotique voilée, Meret Oppenheim à la presse chez Louis
Marcoussis (1933) © Man Ray Trust/SOCAN (2021).

The image in Figure 5 from the series, titled *Erotique Voilée* was
published in the surrealist magazine *Minotaure* in 1934, alongside an
essay, 'La beauté sera convulsive' by André Breton. In the periodical,

the image of Oppenheim appears alongside other photographs by Man Ray and Brassai of corals, salt crystals, geodes, abstract figments, playing cards, and sculptures. Breton's meditations in the essay emphasize complexity and contradiction: 'La beauté convulsive sera erotique-Voilée, explosante-fixe, magique-circonstancielle, ou ne sera pas' (16).[104] The combined effect of images and text is glittery and destabilizing, at once organic and unnatural. In Breton's framework, beauty and aesthetics are inherently paradoxical, and in a gesture of surrealist collaboration, Man Ray and Brassai's images are titled after the aesthetic contradictions that Breton articulates in the essay. The title *Erotique Voilée* suggests both concealment and exposure, and the possibility of reading the printing press as a veil is a highly evocative one: rather than elucidating or making accessible, the press here obscures. This image is one of the most well-known portraits of Oppenheim, whose art works, including her 'Table with Bird's Feet' and 'Breakfast in Fur' came to be central in the surrealist movement as subversions of domestic artefacts and fusions of the animal and the human.[105] The fact that she is most often depicted now in a nude taken by a man in another man's atelier has struck some feminist critics as enraging ('peut-être fâcheux', writes Alexandre Mare),[106] since they wish that these photographs would not stand in for the legacy of an artist whose own works were so innovative, influential, and distinct from those of her male counterparts.

In her work on Nancy Cunard's Hours Press, Mercedes Aguirre contrasts the Oppenheim portraits with Cunard's professional and constructed photographs of her printers' identity (discussed later), and reads the press in *Erotique Voilée* as an 'eroticised object dissociated from its primary function',[107] which – while it seems valid in relation to the nudes – is complicated in view of the whole sequence of Man Ray's

---

[104] 'Convulsive beauty will be veiled-erotic, explosive-fixed, cirumstancial-magic, or it will not be' (my translation).

[105] National Museum of Women in the Arts, 'Meret Oppenheim: Tender Friendships'.

[106] Mare, 'La beauté sera désinhibée', p. 153.

[107] Aguirre, 'Publishing the Avant-Garde', p. 285.

images. Within this sequence of images taken in Marcoussis's atelier are a few slightly lesser known photographs, one of which shows Oppenheim fully clothed and actually operating the press with Marcoussis observing sternly in the background. In the clothed image, Oppenheim is the one pulling the prints: yet another reversal of the dynamic of agency and subjection that seems to be suggested by *Erotique Voilée*.

While Oppenheim herself was an artist rather than a printer, her fellow surrealist Nancy Cunard ran an important small publishing house called the Hours Press. I will discuss Cunard's writings about typesetting further in Part 4, but here I include a posed image of her pulling prints. I've written collaboratively elsewhere about a portrait of Henry Crowder and Nancy Cunard, standing back to back in the press room.[108] One of the most striking elements of that image is the inversion of typical gender roles in the shop itself: Cunard is pulling the prints and Crowder setting the type, subverting expectations of composing as work more commonly undertaken by women. In Figure 6, however, Cunard poses in a bowtie and jacket, calling to mind the type of affluent masculinity portrayed in the Kelsey manual. The mess of the studio shelves above her, with stacks of disorderly scattered paper, contrast with the crisp constructedness of Cunard's own image. Aguirre points to the intense professionalism of these photographs, showing Cunard dressed up for the job and seeming to perform its value.

3.2 Subverting 'Man-Made Rules': American Business Owners of the 1940s

While Cunard and Oppenheim represent the world of high art and experimental surrealist literature, the world of fine printing is another domain in which women had to stake a particular kind of claim. Jane Bissell Grabhorn is one of the legendary figures of women's print history in the United States of America.[109] Grabhorn was the force behind one of the most significant collections of women's print work; the collaborative anthology *Bookmaking*

---

[108] Staveley et al., 'New Hands on Old Papers'.

[109] See 'Jane Grabhorn, the Roguish Printer of the Jumbo Press', for a photograph taken by Marjorie Farquar of Jane Grabhorn inking a Washington Press in 1945.

Figure 6 Nancy Cunard printing at the Hours Press. Getty Images.

on the Distaff Side (1937). One of the techniques that Grabhorn used to engage with the male-dominated industry was humour: her printed works often contain a fun and even flippant attitude. In her light rhyming comic ballad 'Jumbo's Lament', Grabhorn expresses her particular combination of attention to the intricacies of craft and her own singular and self-driven approach to printing:

> I have tried in all ways
> To be a perfect printer
> I have never been swayed
> By thoughts of fame or dinner
> I have used white paper
> And I have used black ink
> I have never catered
> To what other people think.

Grabhorn rejected not only the dominance of male roles in the print industry but also the values and aesthetics that were promoted in what critic Kathleen Walkup describes as the 'traditional and staid'[110] world of fine printing (Grabhorn herself refers to the lineage of male fine printers in *A Typografic Discourse* as 'pompous, tottering pretenders').[111] Favouring a creative, funny, and inventive approach, Grabhorn suggested that women could provide a new method of printing that was less bound to rigid principles and, to use her phrase, 'man-made **rules**' – a printing method that enabled women printers to be more 'free'.

Her irreverent style was evident in her formation of an imprint she called the Jumbo Press (1937–73), a space where she could take her skill and training in fine printing and apply it in a loose fashion: 'Fine Printing', she wrote, 'is supposed to be so difficult that only Gutenberg and the Grabhorns ever really did it. But Jumbo has long scoffed at this myth. Jumbo Press says Printing is as easy as the Printer wants it to be.'[112] This construction offers a perspective that goes against the expectation of very structured and rigid exclusionary systems outlined in Part 2, and points to a sophisticated feminist intervention wherein women not only take on roles in a male-dominated industry, but remake printing itself. As Mallory Haselberger notes, Grabhorn's work, appearing on the scene in the 1930s and pre-dating the second-wave feminist movements that would solidify a place for women in countercultural discourses of print, Grabhorn's initiative in printing 'metamorphoses the press as a tool for promoting social change'.[113] Grabhorn's commitment to the cause of reinventing a new kind of fine printing that was feminist, collaborative, and also feminine relied not only on the act of producing prints but also, as Haselberger emphasizes, 'as a form of reclamation of words'.[114] In this sense, although Grabhorn was first a printer and then an author, the inverse of many of the examples I'll discuss in the final part, she too was a literary printer, moved to produce

[110] Walkup, 'Potluck Books', p. 158.

[111] Grabhorn, *Bookmaking on the Distaff Side*, p. 8.

[112] Walkup, 'Potluck Books', p. 160.

[113] Haselberger, 'The Feminist Possibilities of Print', para. 2.   [114] Ibid., para. 4.

works that articulated female roles in the industry with her tongue firmly in her cheek.

A contemporary of Grabhorn, Ruth Ellis, who operated an electrically-powered **treadle press** out of her home, was an American LGBTQ+ icon and an important activist figure in queer and black communities in Illinois. Ellis's business was a dominantly commercial one.[115] Ellis learned to typeset in the 1920s at I. E. Foster & Co., a black-owned operation in her home-town of Springfield, Illinois. Shortly afterwards, Ellis moved to Detroit, where she worked for a time in the printing trade at Waterfield & Heath, an all-black printing firm.[116] Eventually, she inherited money from her brother, and with the support of her partner, Ceciline 'Babe' Franklin, began a printing company, Ellis and Franklin Co.[117] They printed mostly community documents including flyers, stationery, and business documents, and operated the press out of their home.[118] That simultaneous domestic and commercial setting also became a site of inclusion and activism. It was known as the 'Gay Spot' and welcomed African American LGBTQ+ individuals who were often excluded from Detroit gay bars. Of the decision to start her own press operation, Ellis said: 'I was working for a printer, and I said to myself if I can do this for him, how come I can't do it for myself?'[119] Ellis had a remarkably long life and became an iconic activist in her later years. Her personal papers, housed at the Bentley Historical Centre,[120] contain little information about the printing operation and focus mostly on her life and career as an LGBTQ+ activist.[121] She died at the age of 101 in 2000.

[115] For an image of Ellis at her press, see Hawley, 'Meet the Presses: Ruth Ellis'.
[116] For more on the history of African American print cultures (and on the frequent absence of black culture in book history and print culture studies), see Fielder and Seychene, eds., *Against a Sharp White Background* (a contemporary essay collection that approaches African American print culture through the lens of infrastructuralism).
[117] Hawley, 'Meet the Presses', para. 2.   [118] 'Ruth Ellis, Lesbian Activist', para. 3.
[119] Wilkinson, 'The Life of Ruth Ellis', para. 7.   [120] 'Ruth Ellis Papers', para. 1.
[121] See Vloet, 'Living with Pride'.

3.3 Industrial Culture, Linotype, Nuns, and the News

While Grabhorn, Cunard, and Oppenheim – each in their way – represent artistic print movements, literary culture, and fine press operations, it seems crucial to consider the factory setting here as well since the industrial culture of printing clearly continued alongside the more radical aesthetic and overtly feminist operations.

The image in Figure 7, by documentary photographer Lewis Hines, shows a linotype operator at work.[122] Hines is best known for his documentation of child labour and for his advocacy through photography for the improvement of labour conditions more broadly. The complexity and enormity of the linotype machines dominates the image, and it's possible to imagine the tremendously loud sound that all of these machines together would make. I was unfortunately unable to find information about the identity of the subject of this portrait, but the image shows the commercial settings in which letterpress continued to be used into the twentieth century, emphasizing the co-existence of various typesetting technologies even as new advances were made.

One of the other contrasts that began to arise in the twentieth century was the contrast between larger industrial settings such as the one depicted above, and smaller regional newspaper operations often managed and run by a single individual. A short film reel from 1929, 'Eve: Editor, Publisher, and Seller!' depicts a woman whose roles spanned the full print process required to produce a local newspaper (Figure 8). The film begins by introducing 'Eve', 'the only complete Lady-Everything-in-the-News-business'. It follows Eve, with short-cropped hair and overalls, writing copy with a pen at a desk, then setting the type on, then pulling her prints on a pedal-operated treadle press, then selling the paper on the 'wide-open streets'.

The footage was included in the cinemagazine produced by British Pathé, 'Eve and Everybody's Film Review', which ran between 1921 and 1933.[123]

---

[122] There is a rich and interesting history of typing as feminized labour. For an engaging example that relates typing to craft practice, see Elkins and Adamson, 'Typestruck'.

[123] For a reconstruction of the contents of the Eve cinemagazine, see 'Eve and Everybody's Film Review'.

Figure 7 Linotype operator by Lewis W. Hines (1920). Reproduced with the permission of the George Eastman Historical Center.

The magazine's slogan was 'fun, fashion, and fancy', and this sequence fitted with its pattern of showing women engaged in various jobs, hobbies, and activities. The tone of the short is lively, and Eve is seen both engaged in each

Figure 8 Still from 'Eve: Editor, Publisher, and Seller!' Still reproduced with the permission of British Pathé Film Archive.

task and also smiling gleefully at the end (Figure 9). The overall effect creates a kind of spectacle of her femininity, with the titles and exclamatory punctuation emphasizing the unusual nature of her multiple roles.

No treatment of the culture of women in print would be complete without including a brief discussion of nuns. While the earliest documented examples of female labour in print were the nuns at Ripoli, as I mentioned earlier, there was a continuing although niche tradition of this work into the twentieth century. One such example of an internal convent printing operation ran out of the Convent of the Sisters of Sainte-Croix in Quebec, Canada, into the 1940s.[124] The nuns ran an in-house printing operation, undertaking each

---

[124] For digitized archival photographs of the nuns' print shop, see 'Vanier College.'

Figure 9 Still from 'Eve: Editor, Publisher, and Seller!' Still reproduced with the permission of British Pathé Film Archive.

aspect of the printing process. Printing operations run by nuns during this period were generally designed to allow them to produce materials for the local community including event notices, circulars, and obituaries. Many such operations wound down in the late 1980s as newer and less labour-intensive technologies became available for these purposes.[125]

---

[125] Since many convent spaces, such as the one above, were later converted into educational settings (the Convent of the Sisters of St-Croix buildings are now part of Vanier College, a CEGEP program in Montreal), there is often a lineage of equipment being donated and repurposed by university book arts programs (see 'The Printing Room,' for example).

3.4 #ladiesofletterpress and #printmakingasresistance

Moving into the contemporary sphere, the archival problem transforms from one of scarcity to one of abundance. While we have only a handful of images of women using letterpress equipment from the first half of the century, the letterpress revival of the twenty-first century is driven in large part by social media platforms that traffic specifically in images. Instagram offers an important community of exchange and publicity for contemporary printers, and the #ladiesofletterpress[126] hashtag turns up over 5,000 images. Similar activist labels like #printmakingasresistance[127] foreground intersectional approaches to activist print. In keeping with the transformations in educational practices, these images often show workshops, educational settings, and open community studios welcoming novices to the practice of printing (Figure 10).

Of course, historically evocative though they can be, still photographs have some limitations for capturing the process and materiality of printing. Video offers the sound of the ink against the rollers (the metric by which printers judge whether they are using the right amount of ink) and the movement of the mechanisms. They show the moment of impression in a way that offers a close approximation of the revelation of pulling the print off the press. Videos can show the narrative of the print process, from long slow beginning in composition to the quick jolt of the final product. The popularity of letterpress printing reels (particularly of the sensorially satisfying process of creating **rainbow rolls** of colourful ink) on TikTok and in Instagram is not in this sense surprising.

The video reels of contemporary social media often also capture the joy of process, such as the still reproduced in Figure 11. In addition to the mechanical sounds of printing and the sound of the ink on rollers (like softly undoing Velcro), they are often set to music. Printers in their studios dance beside their presses, grin as they reveal their prints, and offer emotional embodied displays of joy and pleasure. Exuberance is one of the affective features of letterpress TikTok and Instagram reels.

---

[126] '#ladiesofletterpress'.   [127] '#printmakingasresistance'.

inkandpaper_ldn

inkandpaper_ldn Letterpress Workshops // I don't just create beautiful letterpress stationery, I also help others fall wildly in love with this beautiful traditional craft.

In my beginners workshops, I will teach you how to typeset using traditional wood and metal type, mix your own inks and create your own set of gorgeous hand-pressed stationery.

Previous clients have created notecards, printing playful christmas cards and coasters, and had fun bringing beautiful quotes to life.

Each workshop is for one or two people. Have the session all to yourself

Liked by ladiesofltrprs and 165 others

SEPTEMBER 4, 2020

Add a comment...

Figure 10 A community letterpress workshop in London. Photograph by Grania O'Brien, Ink and Paper Letterpress Studio (2020). Reproduced with the permission of the artist.

If there are patterns among all of the vignettes in this section to be observed, they are often about women who undertake the printing process to communicate a particular aesthetic, political, or community purpose. If there is a way of showing flow, that state of intense engagement, the historical images that remain of women and their presses offer it. Joy and pleasure, if they are felt internally here, look to the outside world and to the camera like focus and concentration. These images often show women working, alone and together, with type, with ink, and with presses. The emphasis on women being involved and participating in all parts of the printing process is also crucial: there is an interest in these images of showing the full suite of production processes, from authorship to distribution, as possibilities

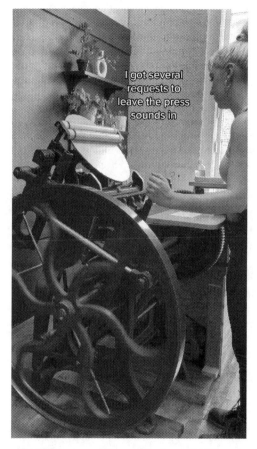

Figure 11 Letterpress process still by Sarah Bloom (2021). Reproduced with the permission of the artist.

for individuals or small collectives, outside of the strictures of a highly structured and exclusionary union system. The means of production are fully in women's hands.

4 Writing

One of the challenges of writing about literature, activism, or art – or really any of the content that is printed on a page – is that the printed words or images are still often considered distinct from the act of printing. And yet, here as with 'impression', and 'form', the language of print becomes obscuring: 'composing' refers both to the act of setting type and to the act of making up a literary work. A **composing stick** refers to the piece of equipment printers use to bring individual letters together, **composition** in literary writing similarly involves the ordering of letters (although it is more common to think of writing as an act of ordering words and sentences). Each is a practice of assembling small units of language into a whole. In this last part, I'm most interested in what I will suggest is a somewhat separate and amorphous category that borrows from a variety of traditions in the service of printing often experimental literary texts: that is, the category of the literary printer.

A literary printer is one who might be a hobbyist or artist without formal training but with an interest in aesthetics and style, and with an approach to book making and textuality that sees the two elements – content and form – as intertwined. Such a connection between text and material is often facilitated through the disruption of the usual highly specialized publishing-industry process in which text-based roles – selecting works for publication, editing, and even writing – are conducted by separate individuals from those who undertake the printing. In the case of the literary printer, these roles are often completed by the same person, by a collaborative partnership, or by a small group that undertakes the whole process together. The examples I mentioned in the Preface of modernist writer-printers working in the early twentieth century – Virginia Woolf, Nancy Cunard, and Anaïs Nin – all fall into this category. So too do contemporary artists such as Ane Thon Knutsen and Claire Van Vliet, whose printed work often returns to the texts of their literary foremothers and authorial contemporaries.

The printers in this category focus on letterpress as an historicized medium with particular relevance to the texts and materials they print. While this category inevitably overlaps with that of the fine printer, the distinction I want to make is that literary printers are primarily motivated and guided by the text they're printing. They have often taught themselves through the informal means described in Section 2. Distinct from the fine press operations that make only extremely expensive and refined objects, the literary printer might produce protest posters, poetry broadsides, political pamphlets, or other texts of personal significance. It seems important to distinguish and make space for this category of printer if academic study is to be inclusive of the full range of letterpress printers through the twentieth century to the present time, many of whom have learned through alternate means outside of apprenticeship models and with varying levels of professionalism and familiarity with trade practices. These printers often produce objects with a range of methods and at a range of price points that might be considered at once ephemeral and aesthetically pleasing, affordable and artistic. In order to understand the lineages that inform the work of this category of printer, it is important to consider both of the types of labour and training experience I outlined in Section 2: the professional printing world and its structures, as well as amateur and DIY approaches to print education. The literary printer often inherits from both.

The embodied cognitive experience of setting type often relates to linguistic production and composition for practitioners in a rather specific way in the case of the literary printer. In other words, it matters to these artists that the medium of letterpress involves letters and words, and not wool, or paint, or clay. This is not to suggest that literary studies and book history haven't had serious and sustained engagements with each other over the years. Writing in 2006, Leah Price remarked that: 'There's nothing new about attention to the material media of texts (from stone to paper); nor is an interest in the movement of stories, their circulation, transmission, and reception, a recent invention. Bibliography, paleography, and editing have been central to scholarship (and not just literary scholarship) since at least the fifteenth century.'[128] Yet, there remains often a fragmentation of specialist fields and subfields within academic discourse that moves the study of printing into a separate sphere from that of literary studies. These circles sometimes overlap, Venn diagram style, but they more often remain distinct and hold competing sets of values that reinforce Cartesian dualism: world

---

[128] Price, 'Introduction: Reading Matter', p. 9.

and body vs. mind and idea. Not everyone, even with the continued development of book history in the fifteen years since Price's assessment of the state of the field, really believes that there can be a meaningful relation between material object and textual content. Even the very injunction 'don't judge a book by its cover' (a bane to many book historians) implies the separation of content and book design that remains a dominant view. What can the typography, and not only that but the physical act of setting type, possibly have to do with the words themselves?

Thinking about printing and writing together in a meaningful way is more than providing historical context for texts. Theorizing the relation between print and text requires a metaphorical or figurative logic, one that binds the material with the immaterial and the compositional with the constructive. It requires a counterintuitive practice of bringing materialism and idealism, those seemingly incompatible poles of philosophical understanding, together. Accounts of printing and analyses of writing have been separated in part by a historical linearity and insistence on a particular kind of non-analogical narrative that resists singular experiential accounts in favour of a broader historical chronology and an emphasis on typical or normative practice. This is an area where literary studies and book trade history still often butt heads. In literature, we consider the exceptional cases: the most beautiful or most arresting poems, the most avant-garde novels, the most culturally transformative plays. In book trade history, the matter at hand is, generally, meticulously accounting for regular practice: describing and recounting what was ordinarily done to make a book and finding out who did the doing. In the past twenty years, a rich critical literature bringing these realms together has arisen, often by taking a famous novel or poem and accounting for its production or publication history and situating the work within its material and bookish contexts.[129] Johanna Drucker, writing of her own letterpress printing practice, remarks on and theorizes the liberalization of language through a paradoxical relation with material constraint that seems to occur in the process of printing:

---

[129] For an outstanding collection of approaches to 'the book' in literary studies, see Gillespie and Lynch, *The Unfinished Book*.

> Handsetting type quickly brings into focus the physical, tangible aspects of language – the size and weight of the letters in a literal sense … Essentially, the norm of language representation is completely reinforced by the techniques of letterpress. Its mechanical design is intended to maintain even lines in a single typeface. But the very rigidity of these norms also permits the use of that technology as a language itself, as a system of possibilities and constraints.[130]

For Drucker, drawing attention to individual letters as the units of language offers a different way of thinking about linguistic and literary constraint and the expressive possibilities that arise from configuring and reconfiguring small parts to make new wholes. Here I'd like to propose an alternative approach to seeing printing and writing alongside one another in a framework I'll call metaphorical materialism. I focus in this part on the work of five literary printers, all of whom have some affinities and relations to literary modernism, and their moments of metaphorical 'seeing-as', or 'noticing an aspect' to use Ludwig' Wittgenstein's terms, when writing and printing form a kind of gestalt and begin to overlap with one another.[131] Like many metaphorical logics, these are often luminous moments of crystallization or clarity rather than ways of reframing regular or everyday practice. The writers I discuss here see differently, even if only for a moment, as a result of their metaphorical apprehension of print. Writers who describe this experience often use the lexicon of print to access something about language itself that lies beyond ordinary compositional logic or linguistic discourse. Women printers who also write the text they print, therefore, or who deliberately print literary texts in experimental ways, are working simultaneously with at least two discourses and sets of inherited cultural values.

---

[130] Drucker, 'Letterpress Language', p. 11.
[131] *Philosophical Investigations*, p. 193.

4.1 Virginia Woolf and the World of Craft

The story of Virginia and Leonard Woolf's Hogarth Press is by now well-known in modernist literary studies and in the history of small presses and publishers of the twentieth century.[132] It began with the Woolfs' desire to create a publishing house whose editorial values aligned with their literary sensibilities. Reflecting on the founding of the press years later, Woolf framed it as an act of refusal: '[W]hen the publishers told me to write what they liked, I said No. I'll publish myself and write what I like.'[133] She began learning to print in 1917, alongside her husband Leonard Woolf, in their home, with the help of a neighbour, Mr McDermott, who was a printer. The Woolfs sought professional training as printers but were denied admission on account of their professional class backgrounds.[134] They purchased their press, a tabletop hobby press of the kind I describe in Part 2, at the Excelsior Supply Company in London. The first literary publication by the press was *Two Stories* (1918) with one story by Leonard and one by Virginia. Woolf writes in her diary that she had not yet written 'The Mark on the Wall' when they had first thought of publishing *Two Stories*, and Hermione Lee notes the relation therefore between composition and material practice: '[T]he new machine had created the possibility for the new story.'[135] The press came first, and the experimental story followed.

'The Mark on the Wall' is itself a story about metaphor and about that moment of gestalt as the apprehension of a variety of meanings and images centre on one initially indecipherable mark. 'The mark', Woolf writes, 'was a small round mark, black upon the white wall, about six or seven inches above the mantelpiece.'[136] The speaker of the story can't seem to identify the mark. At first, it seems to be a hole, then raised substance, and finally she discovers that it's a snail. In Alice Staveley's reading of the mark, it appears as a definitive and patriarchal punctuation mark: 'To an aspirant printer or compositor' the mark might look immediately 'like a period, a full stop, on

---

[132] I tell versions of it elsewhere, in *Modernist Lives* (Battershill, 2018) and 'The Hogarth Press' (2020).

[133] Woolf, *Letters*, p. 348.   [134] Woolf, *Diary*, p. 72.

[135] Lee, *Virginia Woolf*, p. 359.   [136] Woolf, 'The Mark on the Wall', p. 3.

a white page.'[137] A series of fleeting and digressive impressions make up the story. The speaker creates a list of various material objects she's lost, a list that includes, engagingly for a book historian, 'three pale blue canisters of book-binding tools.'[138] Even more than the mark itself, she lights on the seeming unknowability of process: '[O]nce a thing's done, no one ever knows how it happened. Oh! dear me, the mystery of life; The inaccuracy of thought!'[139] Working out how the mark is made is even more difficult, from the speaker's vantage point, than identifying the mark itself. Something has made an impression. But what? The mere existence of the mark seems to speak to a shifting sense of the solidity and contingency of the material world: the mark is at once 'something definite, something real'[140] and yet also somehow indefinable. As the story goes on, the speaker becomes increasingly unsure of her own foundations: 'And what is knowledge?', she asks. 'What are our learned men save the descendants of witches and hermits who crouched in caves and in woods brewing herbs, interrogating shrew-mice and writing down the language of the stars?'[141] The masculine intellectual lineage that Woolf here interrogates collides with a world of self-taught women outside academic culture. Woolf in her own oblique way is here suggesting a kind of constellated approach to intellectual history: the 'language of the stars' can be written only by forming new kinds of discursive and material space.

The early Hogarth books, too, were objects negotiating their own solidity. Like many beginning printers, the Woolfs taught themselves to print and made a lot of mistakes along the way. They over-inked wood-blocks cut by Dora Carrington, their registration is slightly off in many early copies, and the depths of their impressions vary page by page in clearly unintentional ways. They were often unsure of whether they ought to be biting or kissing. One of their other early publications, *Monday or Tuesday* (1918), with its uneven margins and blurred text (more heavily inked on the left-hand side where the roller first strikes the type), shows them as amateurs still learning what they're doing (Figure 12).

The Woolfs did most of the work for these initial publications them-selves: selecting the papers, setting the type, binding the books, and

---

[137] Staveley, 'The Hogarth Press', p. 256. [138] Ibid., p. 4. [139] Ibid., p. 4.
[140] Ibid., p. 9. [141] Ibid., p. 8.

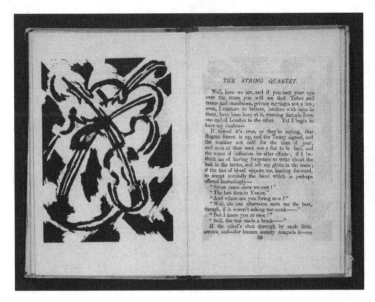

Figure 12 *Monday or Tuesday* by Virginia Woolf, woodcut by Vanessa Bell (1918). Image from the Thomas Fisher Rare Book Library, University of Toronto.

distributing and selling copies. Like 'Eve' from the film reel, they did it all. Her language is veiled and metaphorical, but the process of printing comes into her thinking about language and about making marks.[142]

4.2 Nancy Cunard's 'Fresh and Beautiful' Reading

Nancy Cunard, like Woolf, began printing from a position of privilege. She purchased a hand press with her inheritance (her father was the

---

[142] On the subject of Woolf and typesetting, see Bishop, 'Typography and Time;' Staveley 'The Hogarth Press;' Sorensen, *Modernist Experiments;* and Briggs, *Reading Virginia Woolf.*

business mogul behind the highly successful Cunard cruise lines). She set up shop in Normandy, hired a professional printer to help with instruction and some of the labour, and began to publish experimental modernist works. Before she began the Hours Press, Cunard had published a volume of poetry, *Parallax* (1925), with Woolf's Hogarth Press, and had established herself as an author. Unlike Woolf, however, Cunard was not as interested in self-publishing as she was in producing and distributing the work of others, including poetry by Ezra Pound, Laura Riding, Richard Aldington, and, a few years into the operation, Samuel Beckett. Mercedes Aguirre, in her account of the press's history, notes the difficulty of being precise about the Hours Press given that its records along with many of Cunard's personal papers and her friends' surrealist artworks were destroyed after Cunard's Normandy home was 'ransacked' after the Second World War.[143] What we know of the press therefore comes mostly from Cunard's memoir, *These Were the Hours* (1969). In the memoir, Cunard writes eloquently about the consuming experience of setting type. 'I had decided', she writes, 'to learn printing by hand, as done in the old days. Once that started, Good-bye to all else.'[144] Like the Woolfs, Cunard took on the full suite of activities from printing to distribution, with the help of her friends and collaborators, although she enjoyed the craft elements much more than the commercial ones and reflected in her memoir about her retrospective wish that she had found a commercial partner to handle the publishing business side of the operation.

Along with her friend, fellow surrealist Louis Aragon, Cunard began to learn the ins and outs of typesetting and printing from Monsieur Levy, the professional printer she had hired to teach them. She writes of the sensuous pleasure of printing: 'The smell of printer's ink pleased me greatly, as did the beautiful freshness of the glistening pigment. There is no other black or red like it.'[145] Throughout the memoir Cunard returns to these adjectives – 'fresh' and 'beautiful' – to evoke the novelty she found in printing, as well as the pure sensory and aesthetic pleasure.

[143] Aguirre, 'Publishing the Avant-Garde', p. 274.
[144] Cunard, *These Were the Hours*, p. 4. [145] Ibid., p. 6.

Cunard and Aragon both proved quick students as typesetters, and their enthusiasm and joy in the process rather disturbed Levy, who was uncomfortable with the attitudes and aptitudes of his unconventional apprentices. Cunard reflected on the ways in which the Hours Press seemed to trouble the conventional world of print that Levy was used to: '[H]e doubtless had not yet encountered two such novices as ourselves with our free and easy ways of looking at possibilities, say, of bringing innovations up against some of the consecrated rules of layout "just for the nice look of the thing."'[146] In a sequence of remembered dialogue reminiscent of some of the discussions of the hierarchical apprenticeship system I describe in Part 2, Cunard notes that Levy was keen to point out that Cunard and Aragon would be unable to become 'real printers' since they hadn't begun as boys sweeping floors: 'In France . . . one can't be a printer, you know, unless one has worked a long time.'[147] Cunard's position of financial privilege and power seemed to bolster the strength of her response. She rejected Levy's conventional notion of gender and labour hierarchies, just as she rejected his conventional aesthetic suggestions: 'A new vision, no matter how nonconformist, will also suit the character of some of things that are going to be produced here.'[148]

Unlike Woolf and later Nin's engagements with printing as a primarily or exclusively authorial practice, Cunard's reflection on the relation between text and typesetting take the form of a highly engaged and reverent reader, who was discovering something 'fresh and beautiful'[149] as she subjected a poem to the intensity of typesetting:

I knew [each poem] almost by heart at the end of setting it myself, in the first days of that

> hard-come spring, with its sharp, cold sunsets that marked not the end of my day in the printery . . . An intimate communion with a long, intense poem is already there . . . How much more so when, letter by letter and line by line, it rises from your fingers around the type.[150]

---

[146] Ibid., p. 10. [147] Ibid., p. 11. [148] Ibid., p. 14. [149] Ibid., p. 51. [150] Ibid., p. 51.

4.3 Anaïs Nin's Slow Revisions

Anaïs Nin's acts of printing and self-publishing were born in part of desperation. In 1941, Nin and her partner Golzano More purchased their press and set themselves up in 'a skylight studio [in Greenwich Village] ideal for the work . . . it was old, uneven, with a rough wood floor, painted black, walls painted yellow.'[151] There the Gemor Press began. Nin took the opportunity not to publish new works for the first time, as Woolf, Riding, and Cunard had done, but to republish works that had already been produced, but whose distribution was stymied by the start of the Second World War. *The House of Incest* (1936) and *The Winter of Artifice* (1939) were both originally printed in Paris at the Siana Press ('Anaïs' spelled backwards), but failed to circulate owing to the start of the war. Facing further rejections by American publishers and craving connection with the literary world, Nin was motivated to print by a desire to give her works a new life and to collaborate with More. Yet as the work began, what she found was a deep and lasting engagement with the process of letterpress printing that radically altered her approach to literary composition.

Like the Woolfs, Nin and More were self-taught printers, acquiring printing manuals from the library and reading them voraciously. This was an operation that arose from the impulse to solve a problem of getting her work to the public, the desire to say 'if no one will do this for me, I will do it myself.' It was a way of stepping out of time and conditions, of taking control of the marketplace. But it also became something more: an aesthetic experience born of a new kind of connection to the material world and to language. The solidity and satisfaction of the printing process appealed to Nin, and in her diary are some very direct explorations of the relationship between printing and authorship: 'The press mobilized our energies, and is a delight. At the end of the day you can see your work, weigh it, it is done, it exists . . . The words which first appeared in my head, out of the air, take body. Each letter has a weight. I can weigh each word again, to see if it is the right one.'[152] To read Nin's metaphors here is to end up in a place where tenor and vehicle are barely separable.

---

[151] Nin, *Diary*, p. 180. [152] Ibid., p. 185.

Nin credits not only the tactility and weight of the process with an embodied experience of literary composition, but also attributes the particular slowness and granularity of the experience to a newly focussed and distilled approach to language: 'Typesetting slowly makes me analyze each phrase and tighten the style', she writes, '[t]ake the letter O out of the box, place it next to the T, then a comma, then a space, and so on . . . The writing is often improved by the fact that I live so many hours with a page that I am able to scrutinize it, to question the essential words. In writing, my only discipline has been to cut out the unessential . . . The discipline of typesetting and printing is good for the writer.'[153] As Hannah Sullivan argues, developments in print culture and publishing processes in the early twentieth century created a literary culture that strongly emphasized revision. As Sullivan points out, most writers of the early twentieth century would see their books through the stages of 'manuscript, typescript, galley proof, revised proof, page, proof, first edition', a multi-stage process that already allowed for many revisions and re-entries into the text.[154] 'Mixed technology', Sullivan further suggests, 'produced a high degree of defamiliarization'[155] and allowed writers to re-read their work several times with fresh eyes, each time occasioning further opportunities for refinement and rewriting. Writer-printers printing their own works experienced an additional and arguably even more defamiliarizing experience by adding the typesetting stage to this cycle of production. The experience Nin so vividly describes creates a paradoxically practical solution to the ethereal problems of composition, publication, and craft. By dividing up this experience into single letters, she is also taking apart the big problem of bringing a text to the public and dividing it into tiny, letter-sized, solvable problems. The immersiveness and the embodied nature of the experience is nontrivial. As contemporary book artist India Johnson notes: '[I]ntensive craft training can provide us with the ability to articulate the workings of embodied cognition. It allows us to assert, from the authority of our own experiences, that *how* things are made matters – that meaning does not exist separately from the means of production.'[156]

---

[153] Ibid., p. 192. [154] Sullivan, *The Work of Revision*, p. 38. [155] Ibid., p. 39.
[156] Johnson, 'A Century of Craft', para. 9.

Figure 13 Anaïs Nin printing at the Gemor Press (1941). Used with the permission of the Anaïs Nin Trust.

Nin located her compositional identity in her printers' identity and writes clearly and explicitly about how printing changes her engagement with language also as an editor of her own work. As Emily Larned notes, Nin's acts of self-publishing were crucially also acts of self-editing: 'The opportunity to revisit the text [of *The Winter of Artifice*] brought about a thorough rewriting, and a reconsideration of the collection as a whole. Nin substantially edited the text. She entirely removed the first story, based on her relationship with Henry Miller, making what had been the second story, "Lilith", about her incestuous relationship with her father, the book's primary piece. This story was recast from first person to the third: the "I" became "she".'[157] While these revisions had previously been attributed to Nin's attempts to avoid censorship because of the erotic content and language in the 'Djuna' story that was excised from *The Winter of Artifice*, Larned's suggestion that Nin's revisions were related to her typesetting practice is supported by her generally intensive self-editing practice and her comments in her diaries about the nature of the relationship between typesetting and revision. Elsewhere in Nin's typescripts, similarly drastic revisions (made both by herself and by Henry Miller) are visible as she adapts and revises the texts as she self-publishes: whole paragraphs are struck out, cut in the service of the essential.[158]

Nin's self-publishing endeavour was successful in the sense that all the copies of her initial editions, distributed by Gotham Book Mart, sold; since, like Cunard, Nin was not as much of a business record-keeper as she was a printer and writer, it's not clear how many copies there actually were. She was in some sense vindicated, but the press work was tiring and rapidly became overwhelming. Following on her success, Nin began to receive offers from mainstream publishers, but, as Larned notes: '[T]hey were not asking to publish her stories as they stood. Instead, one said, "Yes, you have great talent. But do you think the next book might be ... more of a novel ... according to orthodox forms?"'[159] Another asked for a novel 'with a beginning and an end'.[160] Nin refused these unsatisfactory offers until eventually Dutton made her an offer to publish without what she considered significant damage to her work. She finally accepted.

In all these cases of modernist women writers who began presses, letterpress printing is taken on as a solution, in some ways, to the problem of market and of reader. How, as an author, does one get one's work out, on one's own terms, to the public? The solution to the problem of

---

[157] Larned, 'The Intimate Books', p. 35.
[158] Nin, 'The House of Incest Typescript'.
[159] Larned, 'The Intimate Books', p. 41.   [160] Ibid.

unsatisfactory publishing conditions therefore requires a refusal of the mainstream market's manipulation of one's literary output (Woolf's capital- -N 'No'). These women's work also marks a refusal of the typical twentieth-century separation between publishing as a profession and printing as a separate trade. Letterpress as resistance craft is very much at play for all these women, returning them, paradoxically, to the kind of domestic publisher/printer arrangement that would have been much more common before the nineteenth century. And yet, as Nin so clearly articulates in her diaries, the act of producing work in this slow, careful, manner creates an embodied connection to language that carries over into compositional strategies. The literal 'weight' of the words is meaningful to these writers, and their engagements with letterpress printing renewed and deepened their commitment to finding and preserving what Nin termed the 'essential words'.[161]

4.4 Claire Van Vliet's Open Books

One of the most prominent book artists of the twentieth century, Claire Van Vliet, founded the Janus Press in 1955 to produce art books that respond specifically through the book's form to the texts that they encounter. Van Vliet, like all the women described in this part, had a somewhat unconventional experience of learning to print and taking up work in this trade. She trained first in Germany, where she learned binding and printing techniques, but when she returned to the United States of America, she found that she had to seek a non-union shop in which to apprentice. She has, through the Janus Press, been a generous teacher and mentor to many new printers and bookmakers, contributing to the kind of educational lineage I describe in Part 2 as being crucial to the survival and development of the craft. Since beginning the operation, Van Vliet has produced over ninety fine editions. Van Vliet's work is not the self-taught amateur printing of Woolf, Nin, or Cunard. It is fine work with a high degree of skill. However, what aligns the work of the Janus Press with the work I discuss here is her experimentalism with the form of the book itself and the direct relation between text and object that informs

---

[161] Nin, *Diary*, p. 192.

its design. As Ruth Fine writes in her bibliography of Janus, 'the book as a balanced and unified statement, with all of its parts integral and serving to illuminate one another, is the ideal after which the press seeks.'[162] The mythic figure of the Janus also represents a way of finding the modern and also the historical in bookmaking, a balance of experiment and tradition-alism: 'For Van Vliet, the Janus symbol also stands both for traditional books, a yet unexhausted form by which to communicate visual-literary ideas, and experimental works as well.'[163] Van Vliet is known for her innovative structures that manipulate the form of the codex through highly skilled applications of non-adhesive bindings and innovative fold-ing structures (often Janus Press books can be hung on the wall in multiple orientations, or folded out into long accordions). She prints on a Vandercook press in her studio in Vermont.

When it comes to critical treatments of the genre of artists' books specifically, there has remained a strong critical and disciplinary divide between literary history and the history of graphic design and typography. As James Sullivan notes, writing of book artist Claire Van Vliet's printing of Denise Levertov's poem 'Batterers', the discipline of literary studies seldom considers artists' books, while art historians:

> [A]tten[d] to the book primarily as an art object –
> a sculptural object or the product of a printer's art rather
> than as a literary object. Such studies tend to focus on the
> development of the visual art genre and do not generally
> attend in detail to the texts they convey. Conversely, scho-
> lars of modern poetry typically attend to text as though it has
> no body ... attending to the words as though they do not
> arrive to readers through some material form, but rather as
> immaterial linguistic constructs.[164]

While the rise of book history and new formalisms of the kind proposed by Caroline Levine could perhaps temper the claim that literary scholars tend

---

[162] Fine, *Janus Press*, p. 5. [163] Ibid.
[164] Sullivan, 'A Poem is a Material Object', p. 1.

not to consider materiality, it remains true that the passage from meaning to materiality remains an unstable and difficult bridge to cross. Especially tricky is the middle space of literary experimental publications. The divide between art history and graphic design research and literary research often remains.

For the artists themselves, however, there is no such separation between text and material. In her essay 'Thoughts on Bookmaking', Van Vliet posits an interactive material aesthetics for the book, which she engages artistically with further innovation and spatial play:

> All the physical components of a book can act as facilitators for the essence of the text. They can engage the senses and widen the comprehension of the text – ideally, without interfering in any way ... The hands will hold it and feel it – soft, hard, rough, smooth, heavy, light – during the time the book is being 'read'.[165]

Here Van Vlies posits reading as both an interpretive and sensory experience, one of simultaneously holding an object and noticing its textures while also engaging it as a text and therefore as a form of thinking. One example of Van Vliet's integrated textual and visual practice is an edition of Margaret Kaufman's poetry collection, *Deep in the Territory* (Figure 14).

The brightly coloured book is pieced together like a quilt from a variety of papers and with pages variously oriented. The book appears in a box with loose bits and scraps of paper in a multitude of colours. These fragments materialize the fragments of old quilts that Kaufman refers to in her opening poem of the collection. The speaker encounters old quilts tucked away in drawers or stuffed in wardrobes: 'No matter how carefully you take them up,/sometimes whole pieces fall away – /thin ribbons, a ribbon, a space, a nothing.' The book is designed to mirror that opening of the drawer or wardrobe to find those loose and wayward fragments. Some might fall out of the box, disrupting the solidity of the codex form. The quilts in the poem, too, act as metaphors for the 'shreds, fluff, interstitial tissue' of memory,

---

[165] Van Vliet, 'Thoughts on Bookmaking', para. 2.

Figure 14 *Deep in the Territory* Artists' Book by Claire Van Vliet. Image provided by the Thomas Fisher Book Library and with the permission of the artist.

worn down and yet preserved and cared for. Quilts appear, too, in another collaboration by Van Vliet and Kaufman: *Aunt Sallie's Lament*. Like *Deep in the Territory*, this book consists of colourful paper squares mimicking a quilt. Writing of this piece, Van Vliet suggests that she seeks out poems or texts that might offer a specifically meaningful relation to material books: 'I look for text that can use what I do – that is, books made by hand. A handmade book can be any shape the text needs. *Aunt Sallie's Lament* is about a quilter and her life – she mutters little comments that form a circle – the book needed to show that circle of feeling. It can also expand out to 105 inches in length and show all the stanzas at once. It can be held in the hand and read like a "normal" book too.'[166] The poem's relation to the spatial play of the piece is clear: the text becomes a series of quilter's squares, and the 'mutterings' interleaved with one another also overlay with the different form and shape of the pages in a way that creates a sense of materialized simultaneity evocative of under-the-breath utterances and interjections. The flexible relation of normative codex forms and experimental practice opens up the possibility of multiple readings of the poem.

Van Vliet's artistic textual interpretations and collaborations also remind one, finally, of the potential of print and particularly of books to offer a multiplicity of possible interpretive postures on the part of the writer, the printer, and the reader: 'To read a book is an act of opening – we open it and we are open to what is inside.'[167] Women's approaches to print practice and writing practice in the twentieth and twenty-first centuries epitomizes this openness, finding new ways of setting and configuring type and setting and configuring language to invoke the full complexities of textual and material relations.

4.5 Ane Thon Knutsen: Marking the Walls

Ane Thon Knutsen, a graphic designer and associate professor at the Oslo National Academy of the Arts, began her work in letterpress after a week-long course at Oslo National Academy of the Arts led by Maziar Raein in 2008 and continued on her own until she started a PhD in 2015. During her studies she decided to undergo a rigorous apprenticeship program through

---

[166] Ibid., para. 9. [167] Ibid., para. 1.

traditional craft training. Knutsen had initially thought that for her practice-based PhD research she would investigate the industrial history of letterpress printing in Norway to learn the story of the craft in her own nation. As she began her research, she came across Ingeborg Anna Stuedal, a female typesetter who faced significant barriers to her learning in the trade. Investigating Stuedal's story led her to the conclusion that 'the history of the graphic industry is a study of misogyny',[168] and she couldn't stop thinking about the implications of the gendered exclusions of the industrial trade. Reflecting on her own training, Knutsen felt keenly aware that her own positionality differed from that of her teachers: 'I recognized that my story as a female, self-taught printer is different.' She found her initial ideas about print changing as she herself changed. After the birth of her child, Knutsen felt unmoored from the world of graphic design work that she had known. At a particularly pivotal moment, her PhD supervisor suggested that she read Woolf's 'A Room of One's Own': 'I was consumed by Virginia Woolf', Knutsen writes, 'my new goddess of liberty, appearing in my life at a challenging time.'[169] This realization allowed Knutsen to think of her own contributions as singular and to frame them specifically as feminist: '[I]n my own practice', she says, 'there are no hierarchies.'[170] While she felt she learned a great deal about the technical craft of printing from the men who had worked long careers in industry, it seemed increasingly clear that her own work was different in kind. She articulated a mutually beneficial relationship between master printers who have inherited the skills and affordances of the industrial trade and mostly self-taught women who are forming a new kind of letterpress: if this craft is to continue into the twenty-first century, it needs conventional and experimental approaches to exist alongside one another. And importantly, as Knutsen stresses, hands-on learning in pressrooms is urgent: '[T]he window to gain

---

[168] Knutsen, 'A Printing Press', p. 3.   [169] Ibid., p. 2.

[170] These remarks are quoted from Knutsen's plenary lecture at the International Virginia Woolf Conference 2021: 'Monumental Close Reading: Entering "The Mark on The Wall" as an Immersive Installation: Word by Word, Print by Print'.

this knowledge is closing'[171] as the last generation of printers who worked professionally in the printing industry age into their 90s and pass away.

Knutsen also began to think of the history that informed her own practice as one of an entirely different order from the world of unions and professional industry: 'What tradition am I building off of?', she asked. 'As a woman and an outsider? What heritage is there from self-taught, female typesetters? And what about the ones with artistic aspirations?'[172] In finding Woolf, Knutsen posited a new way of creating an unconventional foundation for her work, not by tracing the story of Norwegian printers geographically proximate with her, but by connecting with someone more distant in time and background but aligned in sensibility. This is a perfect example of another kind of leap of connection and gestalt of resonance that I mentioned at the beginning of this section: a moment in which Knutsen's work connects with Woolf's, refashions it to be seen anew. Not only the gestalt of meaning and materials, but the gestalt of shared experience, struck into momentary clarity across time.

Knutsen was transformed by reading 'A Room of One's Own'. When she was first researching Woolf's work as a printer and typesetter, she traveled to the British Library and sought out the hand-printed first edition of 'Two Stories'. When she opened the fragile Japanese paper covers, she was moved, as I was when I first encountered the Hogarth Press hand-printed works, by the amateurish qualities of the work – more 'punk rock and anarchy'[173] than fine press dignity. Knutsen made herself a studio of her own with two presses and as much type and equipment as she could fit into the space. She began to print some of the most experimental short works of Virginia Woolf in newly spatialized ways, these artists' editions offering visual and spatial interpretations of the stories even as they created a new embodiment of typographic form. In one pamphlet, **'Out of Sorts'**, depicted in Figure 15, Knutsen creates pairs of female printers and puts quotations and images of each in dialogue with one another, marked by **manicules.** Nin and Woolf, Anna Ingelsborg and Emily Faithfull.

Enclosed in a semi-transparent envelope – a material allusion to Woolf's analogy for consciousness in her essay 'Modern Fiction' – Knutsen

---

[171] Ibid. [172] Knutsen, 'A Printing Press of One's Own', p. 3. [173] Ibid., p. 7.

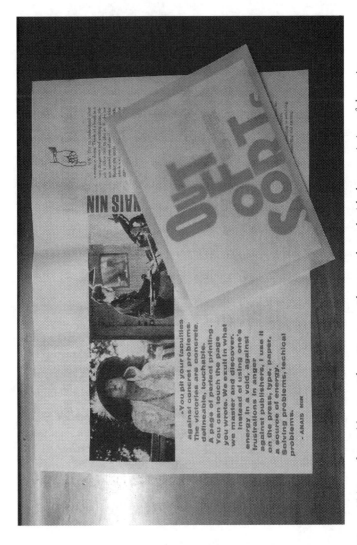

Figure 15 'Out of Sorts' by Ane Thon Knutsen. Photograph used with the permission of the artist.

reimagines the connections between women as a way of writing her own new lineage of self-taught women printers.

In Knutsen's installation work, 'The Mark on the Wall' (Figure 16), the practice of letterpress printing as both criticism and art work is most apparent. All around the gallery space of Overlyssalen, Kunstnernes Hus in Norway, 1,837 single-page A3 prints materialized Virginia Woolf's story. Knutsen printed the text using a Triumpf proofing press, in custom-made Caslon type, printed on newsprint. One word – or small phrase, or mark of punctuation – per sheet, the story filled the whole room: it took up space. Knutsen printed Woolf's story over sixty-six sessions in three months in her own basement letterpress studio. The gallery installation allowed viewers to walk through the story, newly made, and freshly interpreted. The exhibition also featured a performance piece in which Janne-Camilla Lyster, a choreographer and dancer ran through the space, the newsprint sheets fluttering with the movement of her body.

At first, Knutsen admits, she was 'overwhelmed by the size of the room', as she was planning the installation but gradually she came to see the space as integral to the making and embodying of this work. A Room of One's Own, 2017-style. Knutsen also lightly altered the text as she did the typesetting, changing words that refused stubbornly to fit on her pre-determined size of paper. One such revision was 'Shakespeare', which Knutsen replaced with 'Woolf'. These replacements and alterations are also acts of literary transgression: Knutsen confessed that she felt it was almost 'illegal'[174] when she first began to alter some of Woolf's words. As she progressed, however, she gained confidence, and the alteration began to feel not so much a transgression as a commentary on the nature and constraint of type itself. After the exhibition, at the suggestion of a friend, she had the sheets bound into a book, but one that is 'fragile, massive, and impossible to hold in your hands.'[175] This project of reprinting and reframing Woolf's story is just one of Knutsen's engagements with women's print culture from the early twentieth century. She has interpreted this particular story in many different ways through print: by printing the twenty-eight colours described in the story as book-shaped blocks, by printing the 'mark' as various full stop

---

[174] Knutsen 'Monumental Close Reading'. [175] Ibid.

Figure 16 "'The Mark on the Wall' by Ane Thon Knutsen. Photograph used with the permission of the artist.

sorts, and in this gallery-sized installation that fills the space with language that's disaggregated and spatially expanded beyond the boundaries of the codex. Knutsen also documented the whole process of typesetting and printing in a timelapsesequence, offering yet another temporal perspective that foregrounds the embodied nature of printing.[176]

In a 2020 pandemic project, Knutsen breaks apart Woolf's essay 'On Being Ill', focussing this time not on the word as a unit but on the sentence. She set and printed one sentence of the essay per day on a single sheet of scrap paper from her studio through the course of the

---

[176] To view the timelapse, see Knutsen, 'The Mark on the Wall: Documentation and Reflection'.

COVID-19 lockdown that began in March 2020. Each of these literary experiments was specifically and deliberately embodied: Knutsen was attuned to the physical exhaustion of print and documents her printing process to show how these works were made: to capture the immense investment of time and physical labour. She is driven by the texts as an artist and as a new kind of historian materializing literary interpretation as feminist artistic experiment. The texts she prints alongside the words of Woolf, Nin, and others, are her own critical writings about her self-discovery as a typesetter, contemporary artist, and graphic designer with a different lineage from the industrial history of this craft. Knutsen is, at the time of writing, working on projects on printing Virginia Woolf's story 'Kew Gardens' on Japanese Kozo paper and on a new project on Nancy Cunard. This is a lineage of feminist thinking, printing, and writing that allows for experiment and the contingency and surprise of self-teaching. Here, too, is a new kind of historiography and literary critical practice, constructed by Knutsen with her own hands at the typecase.

Coda: Letterpress at a Distance

I want to conclude by situating this Element in the precise moment of its composition: in 2021, over a year into a pandemic that has disrupted letterpress printers and researchers all over the world now for a prolonged period of time. I had imagined that I would make some new letterpress prints myself as illustrations for this book, but the Bibliography Room at Massey College at the University of Toronto has been closed since March 2020. The poetry broadside I had begun to set in February still sits half done in a galley tray, tied up with string. I had planned to travel to special collections in the United States, Ireland, and the UK in the summer of 2020 to see more materials and visit presses in person and to do what I usually do when I undertake a research-focussed book: hold, read, and spend time with historical material. As it turned out, much more of this book than I expected has been assembled and analyzed at a distance, by procuring my own copies where possible, but mostly through digitized materials. There's an irony to this, of course, in a book that talks about and indeed advocates for the importance of embodied cognition and material history, that some of what I write about here I have seen only in pixels and not on paper. That I could do so is a testament to how much has changed about communication and access to materials during the time period this book covers, and in many ways it's a fitting place to end up in: with the bite impression instead comprised of bytes, digital simulacra visible only to the eyes and missing haptic qualities. It was still, I want to acknowledge, incredibly strange to write about some of these printed objects without having held them in my hands.

In late September 2020, I attended the virtual 'Ladies of Letterpress' conference, which normally takes place on site at Central Print in St. Louis, Missouri.[177] Folks gather for workshops and talks and tours, and they hold type in their hands and get inky together. Instead the remarkable instructors put on a suite of workshops and discussions from afar, via Zoom, and we had virtual studio tours of community shops, letterpress businesses, and

---

[177] Ladies of Letterpress: Conference.

printing museums across the United States. It was my first time attending this conference, aimed more at letterpress practitioners than academics, and I had been planning to go in person. It was in many ways a poignant occasion. Many of the working print shops now find themselves in dire situations: unable to run the community workshops that pay their rent and, in some cases, forced to give up their spaces altogether and move whole studios – spaces that were often years in the making – into storage. There were presentations with photographs of printers in colourful cotton masks hauling cast-iron presses and full cases of type onto large trucks and sending them off to lie dormant for a while, until the community that uses and supports them can come back together again. Some printers were still in the process of trying to decide if they should give up their commercial leases and put everything in their garages or whether they should try, somehow, to avoid the immense labour and hassle of moving thousands of pounds of wood and metal and keep everything where it is at a substantial financial loss. At the time of the conference, no one knew exactly when studio doors would generally be able to open, particularly in the United States where the pandemic was out of control, the West Coast had been ablaze with wildfires, and the political situation leading up to the 2020 election felt unbelievably tense. Everyone in this small community of printers was sprinting just to stay still. Nothing about letterpress is quick and nothing about it is easy, and in times like these, it is really, really hard. At time of writing – now that vaccination is on the horizon or already prevalent in many communities around the world – the gradual reopening of the kinds of space that invite and welcome folks into the world of letterpress seems more possible.

The pandemic has also given rise to a certain kind of expansion and democratization of print practices as projects like the Provisional Press have devised innovative manufacturing methods to assist instructors with remote education and to bring printing into more everyday twenty-first-century households. On one of these lasercut proofing presses, you can print with LEGO or type, lock up with paint stirrers or popsicle sticks, and generally make do by using a lot of stuff many of us keep lying around the house. Counter to the hyper-professionalized masculine world of printing, these do-it-yourself and improvised print practices are ones that I embrace as markers of a renewed attention to and appreciation of embodied material work in our moment. Many of the printers whose work is discussed in this book throughout the twentieth century and into the twenty-first were setting type and pulling prints under extraordinarily challenging conditions, their livelihoods threatened by or just emerging from wars and plagues and fires. The fact of letterpress is that metal is heavy, it is real, it is solid, and it is in and of the world, and when material circumstances are unstable, it is extremely difficult to keep going. It's also at once vital and inconsequential: presses can be the engines of thought, historical symbols of free expression and of the circulation of ideas, or they can be hobbies, antiquities, eccentric curiosities, or even emblems of oppressive power and control. In times of crisis or post-crisis like the present, it's difficult to assess how important things like this are now and how important they will seem in the future. The intense care and time and energy that has gone into the preservation of letterpress history should ideally not be lost, and yet there are other grim realities that need attending to, other causes that require more attention and more resources.

Even contextualizing all this within bigger worries, it's difficult to attend a virtual event like a letterpress conference or see a digitized object and not feel a sense of loss. While the marriage of the digital and the analogue that many printers have embraced through the use of hybrid tactics, the strategic deployment of alternative print-making methods like **risograph** and **screen printing**, and the creation of **photopolymer plates**, this is still an act that connects people to their hands, to their minds, and to their bodies, both in the production and in the consumption of letterpress texts. When my hands are at a keyboard and my eyes are on a screen, my thoughts look different, come faster, and are more skittish. If I do the thinking while printing, or even while reading a book with that distinctive letterpress aesthetic – natural paper, shiny oil-based ink, lots of white space – it is slower, more languid, and more focussed. I identify in part with Woolf, Cunard and Nin's writings about printing because I feel some of what they say about the literal weight of each letter even as a reader and as a researcher. So much work and time went into each mark on the page, and any printer who has **pied** a case or even just a line of type will also know that the process is not all meditative contemplation: it's a good deal of frustration and physical exhaustion, too. Whenever I have introduced letterpress for the first time to students or interested passersby of the Bibliography Room, they often see this intense particularity right away as they struggle to grasp a tiny **8pt** 'e' between their thumb and index finger. Sometimes they're horrified ('whole 500-page novels used to be made like *that*?!') but more often they come away with a sense of quiet respect and astonishment. Producing a page of print, which seems so easy now, was once really, really slow and demanding. And some people still do it that way; as a labour of love, as a political act, even, sometimes, against their own good judgment.

We can hope the world of letterpress is in its current state of suspended animation temporarily, and before too long community print shops will once again be welcoming diverse audiences, redefining and expanding the reach of these traditionally white male spaces, and opening their doors to the public. When a colleague and I were speculating recently about when we would next be able to get students in to see the presses and to pull prints, we both ended the conversation with a sort of defeated shrug and a resigned acknowledgment of the uncertain future. 'I guess all we can do in the meantime', I found myself saying, with that specifically terrible humour born of such circumstances, 'is press on'.

Glossary

Bite

The impression that occurs when the pressure of a press is set heavily enough to emboss the type into the paper. Also a common feature of impression on 'damped' paper.

Body Text

The main text of a book, excluding headings, footnotes, titles, or illustrations.

Chase

The metal frame into which type is locked for printing.

Composing Stick

A metal holder into which type and leading are temporarily placed to make up individual lines of text. These lines are then transferred onto the stone and combined.

Composing/Typesetting

The arrangement of type for printing, word by word and line by line. Hand composition is done with a composing stick, into which individual types from one or more cases are placed. Mechanical composition is done with a keyboard. Hot-metal composing machines, such as the linotype, cast type from matrices at the point of composition. The linotype casts a complete line (a slug); the monotype casts lines of individual types. In both cases the type is melted down after printing for reuse. Digital typesetting uses digital font files to create an electronic representation of the text, which can then be rendered on a variety of media, such as computer screens, printing plates, or digital printers.

Forme	The name given to a locked up chase that contains type, furniture, and quoins.
Furniture	Spacing materials used to both make spaces and keep type in place when it is set in the chase. These were originally made from wood and later also of metal.
Hand Press	A h Hand presses is operated manually, usually by pulling a handle across the press to lower the platen (the pressing surface) onto the forme to be printed. They are distinct from presses that mechanize part of the print process, usually through the use of a foot pedal action (as in a **treadle press**). On these presses, inking is also done by hand.
Hand Roller	A handheld roller used for transferring ink onto type and/or woodblocks. Usually made out of rubber in the twentieth and twenty-first centuries.
Hellbox	A box of disused type to be sent back to the foundry to be melted down and made into new type.
Ink	Printing ink now comes in a wide variety of types (including some washable printing inks). Traditionally, printer's ink was oil based (traditionally made with **linseed oil**), but there are also now rubber-based options favoured by some practitioners.
Inkball	A traditional tool used for applying ink for printing using a dabbing motion. Usually made out of leather stuffed with wool and with a wooden handle (called the 'ball stock').

Inker or Beater

Person who does the inking in the printing process. Works with the **pressman** or **puller**.

Journeyman

In the context of printing, the journeyman is a labourer who has completed an apprenticeship and is considered qualified to work.

Justification

In typographic alignment, justification refers to the even spacing of the text along a line. Justification can be full, right, left, or centred.

Kiss

The impression that occurs when the pressure of a press is set heavy enough to fully transfer the ink from the type to the paper, but not heavy enough to emboss the type into the paper.

Lay (of the typecase)

The lay of the typecase refers to the arrangement of the letters within the sectioned wooden compartments of the case. The 'lay' varied by manufacturer, historical moment, and location (see Bolton, 'Typecase Lay Selection' for an extensive list of possibilities).

Leading

The gap between lines of type. In letterpress printing, this is done by inserting a thin strip of lead. It is a lower height than the type, so it does not receive and transfer ink onto paper.

Letterpress

A form of relief printing that uses a printing press that transfers the impression of an inked, raised surface of type to paper or another substrate. It typically involves the composition and locking up of movable type into the bed or chase of a press, inking the type, and then the pressing of paper against the type. This creates an impression by transferring the ink from the type to the printing substrate.

Linotype/Intertype Machine A machine to assist with type composition that produces lines of type ('line-o-type') in single strips of metal. The operator works at a keyboard for typesetting. This machine was historically primarily used for newspapers.

Locked Up The term for a forme that is ready to print. 'Locking up' is the process of using a 'quoin key' to turn metal 'quoins' that expand in order to lock the wooden furniture, type, and any ornaments or illustration blocks in place.

Makeready The process of getting everything (type, furniture, materials, and press), ready to print.

Metal Type Metal type is generally made from a lead and tin alloy. It is generally used for all sizes of type except for the very largest poster types, which are cut from wood.

Mimeograph A type of duplicating machine (now replaced for most functional uses by the photocopier) that produced images from a stencil made from waxed mulberry paper.

Movable Type Refers to type that exists in individual component pieces (sorts) that can be rearranged to produce verbal constructs. The earliest examples of movable type were made of porcelain and date back to 1040 in China. Later type could be made of metal or wood.

Offset/Photolithography

Offset printing or offset lithography is a widely used technique in commercial printing. In this method, the inked image is transferred (or 'offset') from the printing plate to a flexible intermediate carrier (often a rubber blanket) and then onto the substrate. For much more on this very complex process, see Kipphan, *Handbook of Print Media*.

Packing

Calibrating the pressure between the press and the printing materials by raising the printing surface or increasing the circumference of either the plate cylinder or blanket cylinder. Adjusting the hardness (or give) of the packing affects the nature and quality of the impression.

Photopolymer Plate

A photopolymer plate is a sheet of light-sensitive polymer that is superimposed with a photo negative and then washed to reveal the exposed area. Plates are then mounted on bases to bring the plate to 'type high' (a universal height of .918") so that they can be used for printing. The advantage of this technology is that it allows any digital image to be transformed into a block to be used in letterpress printing.

Pica

A typographic unit of measurement ('p') that corresponds to just slightly less than one-sixth of an inch. One pica is further divided into twelve points. Picas typically represent horizontal measurements like column width and are commonly used when designing newspapers, magazines, newsletters, and ads. For example, the standard width for a column of text on a three-column grid on an 8.5" x 11" document is fourteen picas and 4 points, or 14p4. Originally just one of several type sizes, it became a standard unity of measurement with the introduction of the American Point System in 1886.

Press Bed
The flat surface of a printing press where the type or printing plate(s) sit during the printing process.

Pressman or Puller
The individual who operates the press machinery (sometimes called pulling prints because of the pulling motion of drawing the handle across the press towards oneself).

Quoin
A wedge-like device used to lock printing type in a chase. These were originally wooden wedges, but metal versions with ridged surfaces are often used with metal type. Typically in a pair, these wedges face one another and are adjustable to different widths to help to fill blank space and keep the type in place when it is set in the chase.

Quoin Key
A small device that works like a wrench to wedge quoins together and create pressure between the coins. This helps to tighten up the type and keep it in place in the forme.

Rainbow Roll
An inking technique in which several colours are applied to a hand roller or the roller of a self-inking press, and the end result is a colourful gradient that requires only one pull of the press. Traditionally, numerous colours of

printing would require numerous runs of the paper through the press.

Reglet

A long piece of wooden spacing material typically available in ½ and 1-pica thicknesses, used to provide spacing between lines, between the title and text or between paragraphs. They are also often used as leading or spacing, particularly with wood type.

Risograph

A type of high-volume digital duplicator-printer designed in the 1980s for printing high volumes of materials.

Sort

An individual unit of type; each one usually represents one alphanumeric character or punctuation mark, or in some cases a ligature (two letters combined to preserve spacing conventions, as in fl or fi).

Spacing

Small pieces, typically metal, that are used to separate type letters and words. Spacing is measured in quad, which comes variations as em quad ('mutt'), en quad ('nut'), three-em space, four-em space, and five-em space. The em quad is the unit of spacing material that is a square of the size of type being used. For example, an em quad of 18 point type is 18x18 points. The en quad would then be half the width of the em quad (9 point wide and 18 point body), the three-em space ⅓ of the width of the em space (common space between words), the four-em space is ¼ of of the quad (18 point 4-em is 4.5 wide), and the five-em space is 1/5 of the em quad (3.6 points wide).

Stone/Imposing Stone	A large, flat stone or metal slab, on which a forme is organized and locked up. It is common for these to be made of machine-ground metal to ensure that they are perfectly flat.
Treadle Press	Refers to a press that's operated by a foot-powered treadle (similar in mechanism to a sewing machine) instead of by pulling a lever with one's hands.
Wood Type	Movable type made of wood, often used in posters and broadsides and for decorative uses. Frequently used for sizes larger than could easily be produced in metal. For an excellent definition, history, and analysis of the characteristics of wood type, see Shields, 'What is Wood Type?'.
Xerography	A photocopying technique that involves the transfer of dry chemicals, which are fused by heat to produce an image.

Bibliography

'An Interview with Kseniya Thomas', *Printing History* 21 (2017), 5–6.

'Ladies of Letterpress', *Ladies of Letterpress*, accessed 1 June 2021, https://ladiesofletterpress.com/

'Letterpress Commons', accessed 23 June 2021, https://letterpresscommons.com/

'Letterpress: Printing Museums', *American Amateur Press Association*, accessed 28 June 2021, www.aapainfo.org/printing-museums.html

'Man Ray (1890–1976): Lot Essay', *Christie's*, accessed 2 June 2021, www.christies.com/lot/lot-man-ray-1890-1976-erotique-voilee-1933-4479050/?

'Meret Oppenheim: Tender Friendships', *National Museum of Women in the Arts*, Exhibition, 26 April to 14 September 2014, accessed 12 June 2021, https://nmwa.org/exhibitions/meret-oppenheim/

'Printing Fellowship Program', Massey College, accessed 17 June 2021, www.masseycollege.ca/library/printing-fellowship-program/

'The Printer's Guide Book', *The Kelsey Company*, Excelsior Printing Company, 1929.

'The Printer's Helper', *The Kelsey Company*, Excelsior Printing Company, 1963.

'The Printing Room', Sisters of Providence of St. Vincent de Paul, accessed 28 June 2021, www.providence.ca/our-story/history/ministries/the-printing-room/

'Ruth Ellis, Lesbian Activist', Sagamon County History, accessed 13 June 2021, https://sangamoncountyhistory.org/wp/?p=11403

'Ruth Ellis Papers', *Bentley Historical Center*, University of Michigan, accessed 16 June 2021, https://quod.lib.umich.edu/b/bhlead/umich-bhl–0047

Abbott, Edith, 'Women in the Printing Trades: Book Review', *Journal of Political Economy* 13.2 (1905), 299–303.

Adamson, Glenn, ed., 'Introduction', in *The Craft Reader* (Bloomsbury, 2009).

Aguirre, Mercedes, 'Publishing the Avant-Garde: Nancy Cunard's Hours Press', in *Publishing Modernist Fiction and Poetry*, ed. Lise Jaillant (Edinburgh University Press, 2019), pp. 135–53.

Albertine, Susan L., ed., *A Living of Words: American Women in Print Culture* (University of Tennessee Press, 1995).

Baines, Jess, 'A Darn Good Idea: Feminist Printers and the Women's Liberation Movement in Britain', in *Natural Enemies of Books: A Messy History of Women in Printing and Typography*, ed. Maryam Fanni, Matilda Flodmark, and Sara Kaaman (Occasional Papers, 2020).

Barlow, Marjorie, *Notes on Woman Printers in Colonial America and the United States, 1639–1975* (Virginia University Press, 1976).

Bate, David, *Photography and Surrealism: Sexuality, Colonialism, and Dissent* (Routledge, 2003).

Battershill, Claire, *Modernist Lives: Biography and Autobiography at Leonard and Virginia Woolf's Hogarth Press* (Bloomsbury, 2018).

'The Hogarth Press', *Publishing Modernist Fiction and Poetry*, ed. Lise Jaillant (Edinburgh, 2019).

Beins, Agatha and Julie R. Enzer, '"We Couldn't Get Them Printed", So We Learned to Print: *Ain't I a Woman* and the Iowa City Women's Press', *Frontiers: A Journal of Women's Studies* 34.2 (2013), 186–221.

Benjamin, Walter, 'The Work of Art in the Age of Its Technological Reproducibility', in *The Work of Art in the Age of Its Technological Reproducibility, and Other Writings on Media*, ed. Michael W. Jennings, Brigid Doherty, and Thomas Y. Levin ; trans., Edmund Jephcott et al. (Harvard University Press, 2008).

Biggs, Mary, 'Neither Printer's Wife Nor Widow: American Women in Typesetting, 1830–1950', *Library Quarterly: Information, Community, Policy* 50.4 (1980), 431–52.

Bishop, Ted, 'From Typography to TIME: Producing Virginia Woolf', *Proceedings of the 1995 Virginia Woolf Conference*, ed. Beth Rigel Daugherty and Eileen Barrett (Pace University Press, 1996), pp. 50–63.

Blassingame, Tia, 'Book/Print Artist/Scholar of Color Collective', accessed 9 October 2021, www.bookprintcollective.com

Bolton, David, 'Typecase Lay Selection', accessed 3 December 2021, www.alembicpress.co.uk/Alembicprs/SELCASE.HTM

Börjel, Ida, 'The Vampire and the Darling Priest of Modernism', in *A Messy History of Women in Printing and Typography*, ed. Maryam Fanni, Matilda Flodmark & Sara Kaaman, Occasional Papers.

Breton, André, 'La beauté sera convulsive', in *Minotaure* (1934).

Briggs, Julia, *Reading Virginia Woolf* (Edinburgh University Press, 2006).

Bright, Betty, 'Handwork and Hybrids: Recasting the Craft of Letterpress Printing', in *Extra/Ordinary: Craft and Contemporary Art*, ed. Maria Elena Buszek (Duke University Press, 2011).

Bromage, Sarah and Helen William, 'Materials, Technology, and the Printing Industry', in *The Cambridge History of the Book in Britain*, ed. Andrew Nash, Claire Squires, and Ian Willison (Cambridge University Press, 2019).

Bromberg, Leora, Stephen Sword, Joel Vaughan et al., 'An Introduction to Letterpress Printing', The Bibliography Room, Massey College, accessed 27 June 2021, https://youtu.be/PpWct5TviSI

Brown, Sarah, Regan Detweiler, and Ben Townsend, 'Proof: A Letterpress Podcast', accessed 7 June 2021, www.proofletterpresspodcast.com/

Burr, Christina, 'Defending the Art Preservative: Class and Gender Relations in the Printing Trade Unions 1850–1914', *Labour* 31 (1993), 47–73.

Cadman, Eileen, Gail Chester, and Agnes Pivot, *Rolling Our Own: Women as Printers, Publishers, and Distributors* (Minority Press Group, 1981).

Caws, Mary Ann, 'Ladies Shot and Painted: Female Embodiment in Surrealist Art', in *The Expanding Discourse: Feminism and Art History* (Routledge, 1992).

Chartier, Roger, *The Author's Hand and the Printer's Mind: Transformations of the Written Word in Early Modern Europe* (Polity, 2013).

Cockburn, Cynthia, *Brothers: Male Dominance and Technological Change*, rev. ed. (Pluto, 1991).

Coker, Cait, 'Gendered Spheres: Theorizing Space in the English Printing House', *Seventeenth Century* 33(3) (2018), 323–36.

Coker, Cait and Kate Ozment, 'Women in Book History Bibliography: A Bibliography', accessed 14 June 2021, www.womensbookhistory .org/

Cunard, Nancy, *These Were The Hours: Memories of My Hours Press, Reanville and Paris, 1928–31* (Southern Illinois University Press, 1969).

Daly, Ciara, 'Women of the Cuala Press', accessed 3 December 2021, www .tcd.ie/library/manuscripts/blog/2020/12/women-of-the-cuala-press/

Darnton, Robert, 'What Is the History of Books?', *Daedalus* 111.3 (1982), 65–83.

"'What Is the History of Books?" Revisited', *Modern Intellectual History* 4.3 (2007), 495–508.

Davidson, Rebecca W., *Unseen Hands: Women Printers, Binders, and Book Designers* (Princeton University LIbrary Press, 2005).

DeGaine, Lauren Elle, 'The "eBay Archive": Recovering Early Women Type Designers', *Modernism/Modernity Print Plus* (2019), accessed 20 May 2021, https://modernismmodernity.org/forums/posts/ebay-archive

Denzer, Ben, 'Artists' Books: Examples and Methods', unpublished lecture, Center for Book Arts, New York, via Zoom (2021).

Drucker, Johanna, 'Letterpress Language: Typography as a Medium for the Visual Representation of Language', *Leonardo* 17.1 (1984), 8–16.

The Visible Word: Experimental Typography and Modern Art, 1909–1923 (University of Chicago Press, 1994).

The Century of Artists' Books (Granary Books, 2004).

Elkins, Amy E. and Glenn Adamson, 'Typestruck: On Women and Writing Machines', *Modernism/Modernity Print Plus* 5.2 (2020), accessed 2 March 2021, https://modernismmodernity.org/forums/posts/elkins-adamson-typestruck

Engel, Jean, 'Why Feminist Printers?', *Feminist Collections: Women's Studies Library Resources in Wisconsin* 4.3 (1983), 5–10.

Evangelestia-Doughety, Tamar, Leslie Howsam, Brenda Marston, Kate Ozment, and Sarah Werner, 'Building Better Book Feminisms', *The Bibliographical Society of America*, accessed 8 December 2020, www.youtube.com/watch?v=M3vb-njdwnE&ab_channel=TheBibliographicalSocietyofAmerica

Ezell, Margaret J. M., *Writing Women's Literary History* (Johns Hopkins University Press, 1993).

Fanni, Maryam, Matilda Flodmark, and Sara Kaaman, eds., 'Excerpt from a Conversation with Former Typesetter Gail Cartmail', *Natural Enemies of Books: A Messy History of Women in Printing and Typography* (Occasional Papers, 2020).

Fielder, Brigitte and Jonathan Seychene, eds., *Against a Sharp White Background* (University of Madison-Wisconsin Press, 2019).

Fine, Ruth, *The Janus Press: Fifty Years* (University of Vermont Libraries, 2006).

Ford, Margaret Lane, 'Types and Gender: Ann Franklin, Colonial Printer', in *A Living of Words: American Women in Print Culture*, ed. Albertine, Susan L. (University of Tennessee Press, 1995).

Galey, Alan, 'Looking for a Place to Happen: Collective Memory, Digital Music Archiving, and the Tragically Hip', *Archivaria* 86 (Fall 2018), 6–43.

Garst, Steve and Liz Garst, 'The Provisional Press', accessed 20 June 2021, www.provisionalpress.com/

Gaskell, Philip, *A New Introduction to Bibliography* (Oak Knoll, 1972).

Gates, G. Evelyn, ed., 'Woman's Year Book 1923–1924' (Women's Printing Society, 1924).

Gifford, Lewis, *The Yeats Sisters and the Cuala* (Irish Academic Press, 1994).

Gillespie, Alexandra and Deidre Lynch, eds., *The Unfinished Book* (Oxford University Press, 2021).

Grabhorn, Jane, ed., *Bookmaking on the Distaff Side* (Jumbo Press, 1937).
    'A Typografic Discourse', *Bookmaking on the Distaff Side* (Jumbo Press, 1937).

Haselberger, Mallory, 'The Feminist Possibilities of Print: Jane Grabhorn's Jumbo Press', *The Alphabettes*, accessed 20 June 2021, www.alphab ettes.org/the-feminist-possibilities-of-print-jane-grabhorns-jumbo-press/

Hawley, Kyle, 'Meet the Presses: Ruth Ellis', *Letterpress Play*, accessed 12 June 2021, https://letterpressplay.com/blogs/blog/meet-the-presses-ruth-ellis-detroit-printer-and-black-lgbtq-icon

Holmberg, Karen, 'Case Studies: How a Generation of Women Came to Print', *Making Impressions: Women in Printing and Publishing*, ed. Cathleen A. Baker and Rebecca M. Chung (Legacy, 2020).

Howsam, Leslie, 'In My View: Women and Book History', *SHARP News* 7.4 (1998), 1–2.

Hugill-Fontanel, Amelia, 'Impression', Letterpress Commons, accessed 27 June 2021, https://letterpresscommons.com/impression/.

Ing, Elis and Lauren Williams, 'At the Helm but Unheard: Exploring Women Printers in the Special Collections of McGill Library',

Bibliographical Society of Canada, unpublished conference presentation (2021).

Johnson, India, 'A Century of Craft', *College Book Art Association*, 15 October 2018, accessed 21 June 2021, www.collegebookart.org/bookarttheory/6720805

King, Julia, 'Grab an Apron and Get to Work: Experiential Learning at Massey College', *Devil's Artisan* 84 (2019), 68–79.

Kipphan, Helmut, *Handbook of Print Media: Technologies and Production Methods* (Springer, 2001).

Kopley, Emily, *Virginia Woolf and Poetry* (Oxford University Press, 2021).

Knutsen, Ane Thon, 'A Printing Press of One's Own' (2017).

    'En Egen Trykkpresse', PhD dissertation (2020), Oslo Academy of the Arts, accessed 28 June 2021, www.researchcatalogue.net/view/598364/602024

    'Monumental Close Reading: Entering "The Mark on the Wall" as an Immersive Installation – Word by Word, Print by Print', unpublished keynote lecture, International Virginia Woolf Conference (2021).

Lankes, J. J., *Woodcut Manual* (Crown, 1932).

Larned, Emily, 'The Intimate Books of Anaïs Nin: Diarist as Letterpress Printer', *Openings: Studies in Book Art* 2.1 (2018), 32–47.

Lee, Hermione, *Virginia Woolf* (Random House, 1997).

Levine, Caroline, *Forms: Whole, Rhythm, Hierarchy* (Princeton University Press, 2017).

Levy, Michelle, 'Do Women Have a Book History?', *Studies in Romanticism* 53 (2014), 297–317.

Lubelski, Sarah, 'A Gentlewoman's Profession: The Emergence of Feminized Publishing at Richard Bentley and Son, 1858–1898', unpublished PhD thesis, University of Toronto (2019).

Mare, Alexandre, 'La beauté sera désinhibée (à propos de Meret Oppenheim)', *Revues des deux mondes* (May 2014).

Maruca, Lisa M., 'Bodies of Type: The Work of Textual Production in English Printers' Manuals', *Eighteenth Century Studies* 36.3 (2003), 321–43.

Maxwell, John, 'Coach House Press in the Early Digital Period', *Devil's Artisan* 77 (2015), 1–7.

McDonald, J.Ramsay, *Women in the Printing Trades: A Sociological Study* (King & Son, 1904).

Metcalf, Bruce, 'The Hand: At the Heart of Craft', accessed 12 June 2021, www.brucemetcalf.com/the-hand-at-the-heart-of-craft

Moog, Christine N., 'Women and Widows: Invisible Printers', in *Making Impressions: Women in Printing and Publishing*, ed. Cathleen A. Baker and Rebecca M. Chung (Legacy, 2020).

Mowris, Lennie Gray, 'What I Learned Designing Intersectional Feminism as a Letterpress Studio', *Medium*, 6 November 2019, accessed 20 June 2021, https://lenspeace.medium.com/what-i-learned-designing-intersectional-feminism-as-a-letterpress-studio-93173ad3f820

Moxon, Joseph, *Mechanick Exercises; or, The Doctrine of Handy-works* (Rose & Crown, 1685).

Murray, Simone, '"Deeds and Words": The Woman's Press and the Politics of Print', *Women: A Cultural Review* 11.3 (2000), 197–222.

News on Screen, 'Eve And Everybody's Film Review', accessed 28 June 2021, http://bufvc.ac.uk/newsonscreen/search/index.php/series/80

Ní Bheacháin, Caoilfhion, 'The Dun Emer Press', *The Modernist Archives Publishing Project*, accessed 2 June 2021, www.modernistarchives.com/business/the-dun-emer-press

Nin, Anaïs, *Diary of Anaïs Nin Volume Three: 1939–44* (Harcourt & Brace, 1969).

'The House of Incest' Typescript, McCormick Special Collections and Archives, Northwestern University.

Olson, Tillie, *Silences* (Feminist Press, 1978; 25th anniversary edition, 2003).

Ozment, Kate, 'Rationale for Feminist Bibliography', *Textual Cultures* 31.1 (2020), 149–78.

Peat, Alexandra, 'A Word to Start an Argument With: Virginia Woolf's Craftsmanship', *Women: A Cultural Review* 32 (2021), 32–51.

Pressman, Jessica, *Bookishness: Loving Books in a Digital Age* (Columbia University Press, 2020).

Price, Leah, 'Introduction: Reading Matter', *PMLA*, 121.1 (2006), 9–16.

Pye, David, *The Nature of Art and Workmanship* (Cambridge University Press, 1968).

Ransom, Will, *Private Presses and Their Books* (R.R. Bowker Co., 1929).

Reynolds, Sian, *Britannica's Typesetters: Women Compositors in Edwardian Edinburgh* (Edinburgh University Press, 1989).

Roman, Dianne L., 'Detangling the Medusa in Early American Printing History', *Making Impressions: Women in Printing and Publishing*, ed. Cathleen A. Baker and Rebecca M. Chung (Legacy, 2020).

Ruggie Saunders, Cathie and Martha Chiplis, *For the Love of Letterpress: A Printing Handbook for Instructors and Students* (Bloomsbury, 2013).

Rundsfeld, Alan, 'The Excelsior Press Museum and Print Shop', accessed 3 December 2021, www.excelsiorpress.org/

Salesses, Matthew, *Craft in the Real World: Rethinking Fiction Writing and Workshopping* (Catapult, 2021).

Shields, David, 'What is Wood Type?', *Hamilton Wood Type*, accessed 29 June 2021, https://woodtype.org/pages/what-is-wood-type

Skelton, Judith, *A Meeting of Minds: The Massey College Story* (University of Toronto Press, 2015).

Sloenecker, Blake, *A New Dawn for the New Left: Liberation News Service, Montague Farm, and the Long Sixties* (Palgrave Macmillan, 2012).

Smith, Helen, *Grossly Material Things: Women and Book Production in Early Modern England* (Oxford University Press, 2012).

Sorensen, Jennifer, *Modernist Experiments in Genre, Media, and Transatlantic Print Culture* (Routledge, 2019).

Staveley, Alice, '"My Compositor's Work": Virginia Woolf and Women in the Printing Trades, 1910', unpublished conference paper, Pacific Coast British Studies Association (2011).

'The Hogarth Press', in *The Oxford Handbook of Virginia Woolf*, ed. Ann E. Fernald (Oxford University Press, 2021).

Staveley Alice, Claire Battershill, Matthew Hannah et al., 'New Hands on Old Papers: Modernist Publishing and the Archival Gaze' *Modernism/modernity Print+* 5.3 (2020).

Stein, Jesse Adams, *Hot Metal: Material Culture and Tangible Labour* (Manchester University Press, 2016).

Striphas, Ted, *The Late Age of Print: Everyday Book Culture from Consumerism to Control* (Columbia University Press, 2011).

Sullivan, Hannah, *The Work of Revision* (Harvard University Press, 2013).

Sullivan, James D., 'A Poem Is a Material Object: Claire Van Vliet's Artists Books and Denise Levertov's "Batterers"' *Humanities* 8.3 (2019), 1–13.

Tidcombe, M., *Women Bookbinders, 1880–1920* (Oak Knoll, 1996).

Van Vliet, Claire, 'Thoughts on Bookmaking', *Poets House*, 10 October 2019, accessed 10 June 2021, https://poetshouse.org/thoughts-on-bookmaking-by-claire-van-vliet-of-the-janus-press/

Veguillas, Elena, 'Women in Type Bibliography', *The Alphabettes*, 1 April 2020, accessed 15 June 2021, www.alphabettes.org/women-in-type-bibliography/

Vloet, Katie, 'Living with Pride', *Bentley Historical Center Magazine*, University of Michigan, accessed 23 June 2021, https://bentley.umich.edu/news-events/magazine/living-with-pride/

Walkup, Kathleen, 'Potluck Books & the Women of the Distaff Side', *Making Impressions: Women in Printing and Publishing*, ed. Cathleen A. Baker and Rebecca M. Chung (Legacy, 2020).

Wall, Wendy, *The Imprint of Gender: Authorship and Publication in the English Renaissance* (Cornell University Press, 1993).

Weber, Marshall, ed., *Freedom of the Presses: Artists' Books in the Twenty-First Century* (Booklyn, 2019).

Werner, Sarah, 'Working Towards a Feminist Print History' preprint, *Printing History*, 2020, accessed 20 April 2020, http://dx.doi.org/10.17613/jb99-v421

Wesbrook, Steve and James Ryan, *Beyond Craft: An Anti-Handbook for Creative Writers* (Bloomsbury, 2020).

Wieser, Barb, 'Women's Printshops and Typesetting', *Feminist Collections* 4.3 (1983), 9.

Wikander, Ulla, 'The Battle Between Men and Women in the Typography Trade', in *Natural Enemies of Books: A Messy History of Women in Printing and Typography*, ed. Maryam Fanni, Matilda Flodmark, and Sara Kaaman (Occasional Papers, 2020).

Wilkinson, Kathleen, 'The Life of Ruth Ellis', *The Curve*, accessed 14 June 2021, www.utne.com/politics/ruth-ellis-americas-oldest-lesbian/

Wittgenstein, Ludwig, *Philosophical Investigations*, 4th ed., P.M.S. Hacker and Joachim Schulte, eds. (Wiley-Blackwell, 2009).

Woolf, Virginia, 'The Mark on the Wall', in *Two Stories* (Hogarth Press, 1917).

   The Letters of Virginia Woolf, vol. 4, ed. Nigel Nicolson and Joanne Trautman (Houghton Mifflin Harcourt, 1981).

   The Diary of Virginia Woolf, vol. 2, ed. Anne Olivier Bell (Houghton Mifflin Harcourt, 1983).

Acknowledgments

My thanks are due to all the apprentices, devils, and printers past and present with whom I've had the pleasure of spending time in the Bibliography Room. Particular thanks to Lindsey Eckert and Stephen Sword for reading and providing feedback on a draft of this work and Amy Coté and Joel Vaughan for early conversations about this project. It's impossible to write of the Bib Room without wishing to honour the memory of Nelson Adams, who taught me more than he probably even realized, and who is missed so much. Thanks to everyone at the London Centre for Book Arts for welcoming me as a studio member in 2013 and opening up a place to print in London and for the excellent bookbinding kit I've carried with me everywhere I've been since. Thanks to Ane Thon Knutsen for the wonderful conversations and for the inspiration of her beautiful work.

Permissions to reproduce images in this book and assistance in locating copyright holders were provided by: Claire Van Vlies, Andrew Hoyem, Grania O'Brien, British Pathe Film Archive, the George Eastman Historical Centre, Lincoln Cushing, Getty Images, Sarah Bloom, SOCAN on behalf of the Vanessa Bell Estate and the Man Ray Estate, and Ane Thon Knutsen. Copyright for images still under protection remains with the named copyright holders and anyone seeking to further reproduce these images should contact them directly. I thank these estates, organizations, and especially the artists for their kind permission to share these images here.

Many thanks are due to my friends in the Book History and Print Culture Program at the University of Toronto and at the Robertson Davies Library at Massey College and P. J. MacDougall and Julia Warren who supported my research in that collection, and the Thomas Fisher Rare Book Library. Thanks to my colleagues at Victoria College in the University of Toronto for feedback on this work at a very early stage at a lunchtime fellow's talk and for the publication grant which allowed me to include all of these wonderful images. Thanks to my fellow panellists, Alexandra Peat and Beryl Pong, and to the attendees at the Modernist Studies Association Conference in 2019 where I presented some of these materials for the first time. Thanks also to all of my colleagues at the University of Toronto in the

Faculty of Information and the Department of English for welcoming me so warmly as a faculty member in 2020. My thanks are always due to my mentors and former supervisors, Heather Jackson, Mary Ann Gillies, and Andrew Nash, for their continuing influence and support.

Thanks to Alice Staveley and Anna Mukamal for their enthusiastic and engaged readings of a draft of this work. Thanks also to the SWAG and JAWS team and 2020 Wednesday writing group for companionship and accountability. Thanks to the whole MAPP team, including Alice Staveley, Elizabeth Willson Gordon, Helen Southworth, Nicola Wilson, Matt Hannah, Erica Cavanaugh, Helena Clarkson, and all of our student RAs past and present, for providing an ongoing atmosphere of collaboration and feminist community. Thanks to Sheryda Warrener and Heather Jessup for the love and magic of our own atelier. Thanks to all the members of the SHARP listserv who replied helpfully and thoroughly to my rather broad query about sources on women printers of this era. Thanks to the editors at Cambridge, including Bex Lyons, Sam Rayner, and Nicola Wilson for their confidence in and support of this project. Thanks to the two anonymous peer reviewers of this manuscript for their helpful and encouraging reports and excellent suggestions. Deep thanks to Maia Roberts, Jessica Lanziner, and Colleen McConnell, not only for their excellent work but also for the collegial and enjoyable Zoom calls.

Thanks above all to my family. To my parents for their support of my professional life and my curious hobbies; to Cillian, always my first reader, for sharing my love of all things bibliographical; and to Finn and Rosie for helping me find a new kind of joy in making books.

Cambridge Elements ☰

Publishing and Book Culture

SERIES EDITOR

Samantha Rayner

University College London

Samantha Rayner is Professor of Publishing and Book Cultures at UCL. She is also Director of UCL's Centre for Publishing, co-Director of the Bloomsbury CHAPTER (Communication History, Authorship, Publishing, Textual Editing and Reading) and co-Chair of the Bookselling Research Network.

ASSOCIATE EDITOR

Leah Tether

University of Bristol

Leah Tether is Professor of Medieval Literature and Publishing at the University of Bristol. With an academic background in medieval French and English literature and a professional background in trade publishing, Leah has combined her expertise and developed an international research profile in book and publishing history from manuscript to digital.

ABOUT THE SERIES

This series aims to fill the demand for easily accessible, quality texts available for teaching and research in the diverse and dynamic fields of Publishing and Book Culture. Rigorously researched and peer-reviewed Elements will be published under themes, or 'Gatherings'. These Elements should be the first check point for researchers or students working on that area of publishing and book trade history and practice: we hope that, situated so logically at Cambridge University Press, where academic publishing in the UK began, it will develop to create an unrivalled space where these histories and practices can be investigated and preserved.

Cambridge Elements ☰

Publishing and Book Culture

Women, Publishing, and Book Culture

Gathering Editor: Nicola Wilson

Dr Nicola Wilson is Associate Professor in Book and
Publishing Studies at the University of Reading and
co-Director of the Centre for Book Cultures and
Publishing. She specializes in twentieth-century print culture
and literary history, publishers' archives, working-class
writing, and histories of reading. She is currently working on
a book about the British Book Society Ltd (1929–60) and is lead
co-editor of *The Edinburgh Companion to Women in Publishing,
1900–2000* (EUP).

ELEMENTS IN THE GATHERING

A full series listing is available at: www.cambridge.org/EPBC